God Listens

Personal Stories of Answered Prayers

God Listens

Personal Stories of Answered Prayers

BY LORENE HANLEY DUQUIN

Our Sunday Visitor

www.osv.com

Our Sunday Visitor Publishing Division

Our Sunday Visitor, Inc.

Huntington, Indiana 46750

Unless otherwise noted, Scripture quotations are from the *Revised Standard Version of the Bible — Second Catholic Edition* (Ignatius Edition), copyright © 1965, 1966, 2006 National Council of the Churches of Christ in the United States of America. Used by permission. All rights reserved.

English translation of the *Catechism of the Catholic Church* for use in the United States of America copyright © 1994, United States Catholic Conference, Inc. — Libreria Editrice Vaticana. English translation of the *Catechism of the Catholic Church: Modifications from the Editio Typica* copyright © 1997, United States Catholic Conference, Inc. — Libreria Editrice Vaticana.

Every reasonable effort has been made to determine copyright holders of excerpted materials and to secure permissions as needed. If any copyrighted materials have been inadvertently used in this work without proper credit being given in one form or another, please notify Our Sunday Visitor in writing so that future printings of this work may be corrected accordingly.

Copyright © 2017 by Lorene Hanley Duquin. Published 2017.

22 21 20 19 18 17 1 2 3 4 5 6 7 8 9

All rights reserved. With the exception of short excerpts for critical reviews, no part of this work may be reproduced or transmitted in any form or by any means whatsoever without permission from the publisher. For more information, visit: www.osv.com/permissions.

Our Sunday Visitor Publishing Division, Our Sunday Visitor, Inc., 200 Noll Plaza, Huntington, IN 46750; 1-800-348-2440

ISBN: 978-1-68192-093-1 (Inventory No. T1830)
eISBN: 978-1-68192-094-8
LCCN: 2017952712

Cover design: Tyler Ottinger
Cover art: Shutterstock
Interior design: Dianne Nelson

PRINTED IN THE UNITED STATES OF AMERICA

About the Author

Lorene Hanley Duquin is a Catholic author and lecturer. She lives in Williamsville, New York, with her husband, Richard. They have four adult children and eight grandchildren.

To my grandchildren —
Colin, Ellie, Patrick, Lilia, Alaina,
John, Mark, and James —
with the hope that you will grow up
to be people of prayer.

Table of Contents

Introduction 9

CHAPTER 1: *God Listens … God Answers* 11

CHAPTER 2: *"Lord, Teach Us to Pray"* 15

CHAPTER 3: *Come, Holy Spirit* 26

CHAPTER 4: *"If Today You Hear His Voice …"* 37

CHAPTER 5: *Signs from Above* 48

CHAPTER 6: *I Need a Miracle!* 61

CHAPTER 7: *Objects of Faith* 73

CHAPTER 8: *Praying with Our Lady* 83

CHAPTER 9: *Saints Alive!* 97

CHAPTER 10: *Lead Me, Lord* 109

CHAPTER 11: *To Forgive and to Be Forgiven* 118

CHAPTER 12: *Money from Heaven* 128

CHAPTER 13: *Without a Doubt* 137

CHAPTER 14: *Unanswered Prayers* 147

CHAPTER 15: *When Someone Is Dying* 156

CHAPTER 16: *The Prayers of Others* 165

Afterword 177

Notes 178

Introduction

This is a book about answered prayer. It illustrates how Catholics pray in a lot of different ways and in a lot of different situations. It shows how God responds to those prayers in ways that are sometimes ordinary and sometimes extraordinary.

In reflecting on why there is a need for a book like this, my editor, Mary Beth Baker, suggested:

> God is so close to us. Sometimes we have to see him acting in other people's lives to be reminded of that. God listens and more than listens; he is constantly at work in our lives, through our lives, for our good and the good of everyone we meet. This book is a reminder of that fact, and a call to each of us to open our hearts to God in prayer, trusting that he's hearing every word and answering in his own way, even if it's not the way we might think we want. Ultimately, his answers to our prayers are always directed to one thing: to bring us to a place where we can live in deeper union with him.

The stories that you will read in this book are all written in the first person. Other than shortening them a bit, I did very little editing so as not to interfere with each person's account of what happened. I organized the stories into chapters that reflect different styles of prayer. I have also included sidebars with brief explanations of Catholic prayers, traditions, saints, and ministries.

Maybe you are reading this book because you want to know more about prayer. Maybe you feel as if your prayer life needs a boost. Maybe you are just curious about how other people pray or how God responds to people's prayers. Whatever the reason, my prayer is that in the pages of this book, the Holy Spirit will offer you new insights and deeper understanding about your relationship with God. I pray that you will experience the peace of Christ. And I pray that you will grow in faith, hope, and love.

— *Lorene Hanley Duquin*

CHAPTER 1

God Listens … God Answers

God answers prayers. Sometimes, he gives us exactly what we want — but not always. There are also times when God surprises us by leading us down paths we never even considered.

My story of how this book came to be is a prime example.

I was recovering from major surgery, after an accidental fall that required reconstruction of my pelvis and months of rehab, when Bert Ghezzi, one of the acquisition editors at Our Sunday Visitor, called. He asked if I would do a book of stories about how God answers people's prayers. He pointed out that there are many books about answered prayer, but none of them focused on Catholic prayer. He insisted that there was a need for this kind of book.

Writing a book was not part of my plan. I would eventually have to attempt walking with crutches and then a cane. It would be a long time before I would be back on both feet. I had anticipated that I would spend my long period of recovery catching up on reading and watching movies. The idea of working on a book had not even crossed my mind.

My first reaction to Bert's suggestion was not positive. The more Bert talked, the more I started to think about all the work that would be involved in doing this kind of book, and that made me feel even less positive. One of my biggest concerns was where I would find stories. Catholics tend to be private when it comes to their relationship with God. Most Catholics are not known for their willingness to share faith stories.

But Bert felt very strongly that this was the perfect project for me. He urged me to pray about it. So I started praying, "Lord, is this what you want me to do?" I was secretly hoping the answer would be "No!"

I did not get an immediate answer. So I decided to send out a few emails asking friends and associates if they or someone they knew might have a story for a book like this. Within a few days, I started getting responses — not just from the people I had contacted, but from friends of friends, relatives of friends, strangers who had heard about it through the Catholic grapevine, and friends of strangers from all over the United States and Canada. What amazed me even more was the variety of the stories. Clearly, the idea for this book had captured people's hearts, and they wanted to share the way God had touched their lives.

One woman wrote, "I heard that you were writing a book on answered prayer in the lives of everyday Catholics. Thanks for taking the time to write such a book. I wish you Godspeed with the project. I'm sure such a book will be an encouragement to many people."

This woman's note was the final answer to my prayer. I began to see that God not only wanted me to write this book, but that the Holy Spirit was inspiring people to send their stories to me. Some people submitted only one story. Others submitted several. Each story was unique and deeply personal.

But that's not the end of my story! I was very close to a first draft on this book when my editor told me that he would be retiring soon. I was stunned. The idea for this book had been Bert's, and he would be gone before my deadline for submitting the manuscript. Bert assured me that Our Sunday Visitor was in the process of hiring a new acquisitions editor who would work with me to bring this book to completion.

I tried to be hopeful. Changing editors in the middle of a book project is daunting. How could this happen? What was I going to do?

Then suddenly, it occurred to me that I was writing a book about prayer. The only thing I could do was pray! But my prayer sounded more like a challenge than a request. I found myself praying, "Okay, Lord, this is your book. I am putting all of this in your hands. If this book is meant to be, then you will have to make sure that everything works out with a new editor."

Six weeks before my deadline, I received an email from Mary Beth Baker, introducing herself as my new editor and asking if we could set up a time to talk. "I'm very excited to be part of this project," she wrote, "and I look forward to working with you! Please know you can contact me at any time with questions or concerns. And of course, let me know how I can be of service to you as you finish up your manuscript."

I heaved a huge sigh of relief. God listened! God answered my prayer!

WHAT IS PRAYER?

Saint Clement of Alexandria, one of the Fathers of the Church, tells us that the essence of prayer is "keeping company with God." Prayer begins with a deep inner desire to seek God, and it develops into a loving relationship where we give ourselves to God and then respond as God makes himself known to us.

The *Catechism of the Catholic Church* lists five different forms of prayer:

1. *Blessing and adoration.* We can offer prayers of blessing because God is the source of every blessing. We adore God in humble recognition that he is our creator and we are his creatures.

2. *Petition*. We pour out to God our needs.
3. *Intercession*. We pray for the needs of others.
4. *Thanksgiving*. We express our gratitude to God.
5. *Praise*. We honor and worship God.

Prayer Is Good for You

While prayer is important for our spiritual well-being, medical researchers are now discovering that prayer also plays a role in physical health and emotional stability. Recent studies show that prayer helps to lower blood pressure, strengthens the immune system, reduces anxiety, and increases quality of life. Other studies conclude that people who pray seem happier, suffer less from depression, and are better able to cope with life's challenges.

CHAPTER 2

"Lord, Teach Us to Pray"

Saint Luke tells us that Jesus was praying one day, and afterward one of his disciples asked Jesus if he would teach them how to pray. Jesus responded by giving this disciple (and all of us) the profound words of the Our Father (Luke 11:1–4).

The Catholic Church considers the Our Father "the fundamental Christian prayer." Saint Thomas Aquinas called it "the most perfect of prayers." If we spent our whole lives reflecting on the Our Father, we would only scratch its surface. In this prayer we praise God, await the coming of God's kingdom, surrender ourselves to God's will, ask for physical and spiritual sustenance, seek forgiveness, forgive others, and ask for protection from trials and temptations in life.

Pope Francis prays five Our Fathers every night. "In the evening, before going to bed, I say this short prayer: 'Lord, if you will, you can make me clean!' " he explains. "And I pray five 'Our Fathers,' one for each of Jesus' wounds, because Jesus has cleansed us with his wounds."

Most of us were taught the Our Father, the Hail Mary, Grace Before Meals, the Rosary, and other basic Catholic prayers as children. These prayers remain a constant source of spiritual support throughout our lives. But it is not uncommon for people to seek other ways to pray at different stages in life.

Some people look for new styles of prayer because they feel a deep desire to grow closer to God. Others want to strengthen their relationship with Jesus or tap into the power of the Holy Spirit. Spiritual dryness and the feeling that God is very distant can cause people to search for new prayer forms. A lot of people look for new ways to pray when something bad happens, when they are struggling with a difficult decision, or when they realize that they are not in control of their own lives or the lives of the people around them.

Sometimes, new ways to pray come to people unexpectedly. Family members might share how a particular type of prayer helped them. A parish might offer a lecture series on Catholic prayer forms. A friend might extend an invitation to join a prayer group or suggest a book about prayer.

The stories in this chapter reflect some of the different ways Catholics have learned to pray. Keep in mind, however, that no matter what prayer form we choose, Jesus urges us to persevere in prayer:

> "Ask, and it will be given you; seek, and you will find; knock, and it will be opened to you. For every one who asks receives, and he who seeks finds, and to him who knocks it will be opened." (Matthew 7:7–8)

Learning to Pray

My mother was my first guide and mentor into the realm of prayer and spirituality. When my siblings and I were youngsters, Mom taught us who God is, along with our first prayers. She impressed upon us that taking care of one's soul was just as important as taking care of one's body. She explained the rituals of our Catholic faith and, together with my father, ensured that we received the sacraments and knew our Catechism. Best of all, she showed us what it meant to be a compassionate, loving Christian by using the talents God had given her to make a better world around us.

Mom had been involved for over twenty-five years of her adult life as liturgist and organist at our local parish. My father directed the church choir. Mom and Dad used to tell us kids that "when you sing, you pray twice." This is a saying ascribed to Saint Augustine. Now, in my adult years, my bedtime prayers remain the familiar ones taught in my childhood, and the liturgy takes on a whole new meaning when I try to sing my heart out, as my parents recommended. I really believe that my prayers arise to God as symbolic incense and melodic song.

— *Vicki Kaufmann*

HOW CATHOLICS PRAY

The beauty of the Catholic faith is that there are so many different types of prayer. We can pray by participating in the Mass, which is the highest and most perfect form of prayer. We can pray by reading Scripture or spiritual books. We can pray silently or out loud — speaking, singing, or whispering. We can kneel, sit, walk, dance, or lie prostrate in prayer. We can practice meditation or contemplation. We can keep a spiritual journal. We can pray with icons, relics, or a crucifix. We can go on a retreat. We can go on a pilgrimage to a holy place or simply place ourselves in the presence of the Lord in adoration. We can join a prayer group. We can participate in special devotions like the Stations of the Cross, the Divine Mercy Chaplet, the Rosary, or a novena. We can ask for the intercession of the Blessed Mother or the saints.

One of the best ways to pray is simply to talk to God from the depths of our hearts — thanking him for all of the good things in our lives and pouring out whatever pain, fears, questions, or doubts we might have. The ultimate prayer — and almost always the most difficult — is the prayer of Jesus during the agony in the garden, when he prayed, "Not my will, but yours, be done" (Luke 22:42).

I Had No Joy

For the first forty years of my life, I could quote the Catechism and tell stories about saints and feast days, but I never had a personal relationship with Jesus Christ until I accidentally went to a Charismatic retreat weekend.

I had always avoided anything that sniffed of Charismatic because I thought "those people" were crazy. But during that weekend, I got zapped by the Holy Spirit. I learned how to pray in a different way. I learned how to pray through song and verbal prayer and praise. During a healing session, God started healing me from my childhood.

I also met two older women who told me their stories. These women should have been suicidal because of all the things that had happened to them, but they just glowed. I thought, "They've got something that I don't have, and I don't know what it is." They invited me to join their prayer group. I came home and I told my husband, "I don't know if it's my style, but I've got to find out what it is."

I went to this prayer group for seventeen years. What I discovered was joy. Before this, I had no joy. My faith was all about rules. This prayer group changed my image of God and saved my life.

— *Carolyn McLean*

WHAT DOES IT MEAN TO BE CHARISMATIC?

The Charismatic Movement is a form of spiritual renewal within the Catholic Church that emphasizes developing a personal relationship with Jesus Christ and recognizing the power of the Holy Spirit in one's life. Charismatic prayer groups meet weekly for praise, worship, singing, Scripture, teaching, testimony, sharing the gifts of the Spirit, and healing.

"Okay, Lord, You Got Me"

When I was a young adult, I dropped away from the practice of my Catholic faith for a while. Then my brother-in-law invited me to a Charismatic prayer group. They were doing a series on Saint Mark, and my name is Mark, so I thought, "Okay, I'll go."

That night they had a worship service, and it seemed a little strange to me. Just before the prayer group ended, they announced that they were going to pray over a woman in her sixties, who had cancer and was supposed to go for surgery that week. As they started praying over her, I said to myself, "Okay, Lord, if you heal this woman, I'll keep coming back."

The following Monday, my brother-in-law was pressuring me to go back to the prayer group. I was hemming and hawing, but finally, I said I would go. Just before the meeting started, they announced that the woman they prayed over the week before had gone to the hospital. The doctors went over her X-rays, but the tumor was gone.

I said, "Okay, Lord, you got me."

— *Mark Piscitello*

I Turned to Prayer

After my mother had bypass surgery, she became very confused. The confusion came on suddenly, and it was shocking. She would talk gibberish about "bad boys at the bowling alley" and "going over Niagara Falls in wire baskets."The doctors had fixed her heart, but her brain was broken.

The psychiatrist was sure it was Alzheimer's.The neurologist said hypoxia from the surgery, and another diagnosis was multi-infarct dementia. I felt as if I had lost the mother I knew. I cried every day.

Then one day I found a novena at a little shrine. It was a handwritten note. The instructions were: "Say this prayer nine times a day for nine days: 'May the Most Sacred Heart of Jesus, in the most Blessed Sacrament, be praised, adored, and glorified with grateful affection, at every moment, in every tabernacle of the world — now until the end of time.' "

I took the paper with me, and I prayed that I could accept this change in my mother. I turned to prayer because prayer was all that I had. It felt good to pray for help in carrying this burden. I was not alone when I prayed.

Before long, my mother was discharged to a nursing home where another doctor decided to take her off one of the drugs she was on. Her mind cleared up quickly. I did some research on the drug, and one of the side effects was hallucinations. All of the other doctors had missed it.

My mother came out of the fog. She was her old self. This was much more than I had asked for in my prayers! When I prayed, I just wanted to accept what I could not change in my mother. But God answered my prayer with a very big change in my mother. I prayed for one small thing and got another large and wonderful answer to my prayer.

— *Barbara Andrulis*

WHAT IS A NOVENA?

A novena is a prayer or a series of prayers that are offered for nine consecutive days. The significance of the nine days stems from the nine days following the Ascension of the Lord when the apostles and Our Lady gathered in the upper room waiting for the descent of the Holy Spirit on Pentecost.

The early Christians offered novenas as prayers for the dead that were intended to commend the soul to God's infinite love and mercy. During medieval times, novenas were prayed in preparation for great feast days such as Christmas, Ascension Thursday, and Pentecost.

Over time, people in France and Spain began praying novenas to ask for the intercession of Our Lady. Novenas to the saints also became popular and were prayed during the nine days before a saint's feast day. Today, novenas are still a popular Catholic prayer form.

The Lord Always Answers

The Lord lets us know that he hears our prayers. One time, several people at our inner-city mission wished out loud that we had flavored creamers for their coffee. That afternoon a truck pulled up with twenty cases of flavored creamers. They were astounded!

But this is how people come to have faith that the Lord will take care of them. These little miracles help to build their faith. People learn the best prayers are when they just talk to the Lord and then wait to see how the Lord answers.

The Lord always answers as long as we are doing his will. Every day something else happens that helps us to see how the

Lord cares for his people. One of my prayers is, "Lord, let me always have a sense of awe. Never let me take anything for granted."

— *Amy Betros*
St. Luke's Mission of Mercy

ST. LUKE'S MISSION OF MERCY

St. Luke's Mission of Mercy was founded in 1994 by Amy Betros and Norm Paolini, who raised money to purchase an inner-city church, school, rectory, and convent that had been closed by the Diocese of Buffalo the year before. By serving the physical and spiritual needs of the poor, the mission proclaims, through the grace of the Holy Spirit, God's great love and mercy for all people.

"Lord, I Really Need This"

After Mass one day a friend invited me to "Men of Christ," a huge men's conference in Milwaukee. We went to the conference and they were rolling out a men's group for parishes called "That Man Is You." It promised to help men strengthen their relationship with God, with their spouse, and with their children. I prayed, "Lord, I really need this."

My friend and I got our pastor's approval, and we introduced "That Man Is You" in our parish. It was an answer to my prayer!

We have between fifteen and twenty guys in the group. We meet every Thursday morning at 6:00. I get there at 5:30 to make coffee. The first year takes you through how to be a man, and the second year is how to be a husband, and then how to be a father. The sessions explore the issues of our day. It takes what we know and analyzes it, whether it's social science or medical science, and then it takes what our faith says about that issue. Then it looks at how one of the saints handled this type of situation. It brings everything together — this is what we are seeing in our culture, this is what the Church teaches, and here's how a saint handled it. It shows how the Church and our faith in Jesus are the solutions to the problems of this world.

It changed my life. It made me who I am. It saved me.

— *Mike Nuzzo*

MEN'S SPIRITUALITY GROUPS

Since the Second Vatican Council (1961–1965), men's spirituality groups have sprung up in many dioceses and parishes. Some are Scripture-based, and others focus on discussions of Catholic teaching and social issues. The purpose of these groups is to allow men to experience spiritual support and fellowship. Many dioceses also offer annual men's conferences, which feature prayer, music, nationally known speakers, opportunities for the Sacrament of Reconciliation, adoration of the Blessed Sacrament, and a closing Mass.

Go Deeper

I was on a pilgrimage to Ávila, a walled, medieval city in Spain, when I saw a banner with the words, "I was born for you. What do you want me to do?"

These two sentences were part of Saint Teresa of Ávila's prayer, "In the Hands of God." I found myself intrigued by these two sentences, and I felt Saint Teresa urging me to go deeper into my own relationship with God. When I returned home, I searched the Internet for the entire prayer, but after printing it out I could not pray the words. It was too deep, too demanding, too overwhelming.

"I'll work up to that," I promised myself.

In the meantime, I had work to do. I pushed aside Saint Teresa's urgings to "go deeper," and I dove back into my busy schedule of radio shows, writing, and speaking. It wasn't long, however, before my busy schedule came to an abrupt halt. The sniffles I developed after coming home from Spain turned into an upper respiratory infection and a debilitating case of laryngitis. My doctor warned of permanent damage to my vocal chords if I did not agree to complete voice rest. No radio show. No public speaking. No phone calls. No talking.

At first, I was grumpy and frustrated. But after a few days I decided to surrender to the urging of Saint Teresa to go deeper. I took advantage of this silent time to read, and each Gospel reading, each book passage spoke directly to me about the need to rest and be still. Before long I began to crave the silence.

With images of Ávila fresh in my mind, I drew closer to Saint Teresa, whom I have loved since childhood. I learned more about her and about myself. Finally, I was able to read her entire prayer and say to the Lord, "I was born for you. What do you want me to do?"

— *Teresa Tomeo*

SAINT TERESA OF ÁVILA

Saint Teresa was born in Ávila, Spain, in 1515. At age twenty, she entered the Carmelite order. After contracting malaria, she had a vision of the wounded Christ. As her mystical life deepened, the visions increased, and she began to see the need to restore the Carmelite order to its original charism. She established what became known as the Discalced (or Shoeless) Carmelites. During this time, she wrote several books, including her spiritual autobiography and books on prayer. Saint Teresa died in 1582. She was canonized in 1622. In 1970, Saint Teresa of Ávila was declared a doctor of the Church because of the depths of her understanding of theology and prayer.

CHAPTER 3

Come, Holy Spirit

Most Catholics can tell you that the Holy Spirit is the third Person in the Blessed Trinity, and that we receive the Holy Spirit in a special way in the sacraments of Baptism and Confirmation. Some Catholics might be able to list the seven gifts of the Spirit: wisdom, understanding, counsel (right judgment), fortitude (courage), knowledge, piety (reverence), and fear of the Lord (awe); based on Isaiah 11:2. But too many Catholics never think of praying to the Holy Spirit or allowing themselves to be guided by the Holy Spirit. Even Pope Francis has observed that a lot of Catholics do not understand the powerful ways the Holy Spirit works in their lives.

"The Holy Spirit is the one who moves us to praise God, to pray to the Lord, the one who is within us and teaches us to see the Father and to call him 'Father,'" Pope Francis explains. "The Spirit does everything, knows everything, reminds us what Jesus said, can explain all about Jesus.... The Holy Spirit makes real Christians. The Spirit takes life as it is and prophetically reads the signs of the times pushing us forward."

Whenever you feel as if you are being called by God or inspired to do something, it is usually an action of the Holy Spirit. Pope Francis explains that the Holy Spirit "guides us in the way to think, to act, to distinguish between what is good and what is bad; he helps us to practice the charity of Jesus, his giving of himself to others, especially to the most needy. We are not alone!

The sign of the presence of the Holy Spirit is also the peace that Jesus gives to his disciples: 'My peace I give to you' [John 14:27]."

There is no doubt that the Holy Spirit is moving in the lives of the people who contributed to this chapter. Their stories reflect some of the profound ways the Holy Spirit has touched them as a result of their own prayers or through the prayers of others.

DISCOVERING THE HOLY SPIRIT IN SCRIPTURE

Here are some Scripture passages that help us to better understand how the Holy Spirit works in our lives:

- The Spirit will speak through us when we don't know what to say (Matthew 10:19–20).
- The Spirit helps us understand everything that Jesus taught (John 14:26).
- The Spirit comforts us when we are sad and alone (John 14:16–19).
- The Spirit guides us in the way of truth (John 16:13).
- The Spirit dwells in us and gives us life (Romans 8:11).
- The Spirit prays for us when we don't know how to pray (Romans 8:26).
- The Spirit shows us the good things God has planned for us (1 Corinthians 2:9–11).
- The Spirit allows us to experience love, joy, peace, patience, kindness, goodness, faithfulness, gentleness, and self-control (Galatians 5:22–23).

The Holy Spirit Will Guide You

Several years ago, my marriage of nineteen years was over. That alone was enough to test my courage and fortitude. As the weeks unfolded, I found myself scared, confused, and hurt. Why me? I was the faithful one.

Suddenly my self-confidence waned. I had been part of a "couple" for so long. Everywhere I looked there were couples … my parents, my sibling, my friends. I was single now. How would I fit in? I forgot just how much I had shared with my ex-spouse — from the material goods in our home, the parish we belonged to, and the list goes on. I had to start over, but where and how?

I prayed like never before, or at least I thought so. Oh, how I talked to God. "Help me, Lord, to get through this day." My mind was so cluttered.

Since I chose to move out of "our" house, my parents were wonderful, letting me move back in with them until I got my feet back under me. I had never lived alone. I had moved from my parents' home to "our" home once I was married. But now I needed a place to call "my" home.

One day after the divorce was final, I got up the courage to make an appointment with a real estate agent. I was scared to death. A voice in my head kept telling me, "You can't do this. You're much too cowardly. There are budgets, bills, maintenance, and upkeep. How do you plan to do this on your own? What if some noise scares you in the night? Who will come to your rescue?"

As all this was going on, I stopped by my parish to drop some materials off, and I met Sister Marilyn, our director of religious education. When I confessed my troubles to her and told her I was praying, she said, "You are praying. But are you listening? Let God speak, and the Holy Spirit will guide you."

That was THE turning point in my prayer life. All my life, I had been so busy trying to solve my own problems by telling God what I needed. I honestly don't remember ever asking the Holy Spirit to guide me. I went into the cathedral and stared at the crucifix to catch my breath. I felt a calm come over me, maybe for the first time ever.

I don't think a day has gone by since that encounter with Sister Marilyn in the parish parking lot that I haven't asked the Holy Spirit for guidance. "Guide me in helping someone … Assist me in making this decision … Help me to see what you want for me … Let my words be your words…."

I remind myself to listen, too.

As for *my* house … I prayed to the Holy Spirit to guide me to a place I could feel safe, secure, and happy — a place I could call *home* to start my new life. It took a few weeks, but I walked into this house, looked around, and I knew that the Holy Spirit led me here.

— *Jill Adamson*

LEARNING TO LISTEN

Listening to the Holy Spirit is not something that comes naturally, but it is something that can be learned. Start by jotting down, after Mass, any spiritual insights that came to you in the readings, homily, music, or in your Communion meditation. Before long, you will begin to see how the Holy Spirit is guiding you.

It's also a good idea to set aside a specific time every day for listening. Start with ten minutes in the morning and another ten minutes before you go to bed. In the morning, ask the Holy Spirit to guide you through the day. Then empty your mind and spend some quiet time, slowly praying the name "Jesus" until a calm sense of God's presence comes over you.

In the evening, think back on the day. Reflect on how the Holy Spirit may have been speaking to you through people and things that happened. Listening will open you to an exciting new awareness of the Holy Spirit, who leads us down paths that we never would have chosen for ourselves!

The Day We Couldn't Pray

There can be times when a person cannot pray, not even the Holy Name, simply because terror can strike unannounced in a split second.

My daughter and I had spent a great summer day up in the Adirondack Mountains and were motoring toward home in the early evening. We were traveling a flat stretch of highway flanked by high brush on both sides of the road. We were keeping to the speed limit, meeting no traffic, except one car a good distance behind us.

And then, in a flash, a huge, dense, perfect circle of pure fire rolled out from our right, across the front of my pickup truck, and kept on rolling into the brush on the opposite side of the road. It was as high as the engine hood and equally as wide.

My daughter let out a prolonged, horrific, blood-curdling scream, while I was so frozen in fear, all I could do was strangle the steering wheel. Neither of us spoke or even looked at each other until we stopped at the next village to calm down.

Why didn't the truck explode or burn to pieces? Why could I find not even a hint of charred metal on the truck's hood? This huge fire had been right there, flush against us. We thanked God that we were okay.

Some months later, during a radio call-in show, a man related a similar happening in a Midwest field of grass. He wanted to know what it was. The answer was that this was a rare occurrence known as *ball lightning*, when ground-level, high-energy electrical forces come together. But the talk show host never explained why nothing burned in the man's experience or in our experience.

My daughter and I speculated that maybe our guardian angels swept a hand down between an inch or so of the fire ball and the hood of my pickup. Or maybe the Holy Spirit was praying for us from deep within when we couldn't.

— *Elizabeth Fenn*

THE PRAYER OF THE HOLY SPIRIT

In his letter to the Romans, Saint Paul explains that in our weakest moments, when we are unable to pray, the Holy Spirit takes over and prays on our behalf. "We do not know how to pray as we ought, but the Spirit himself intercedes for us with sighs too deep for words" (Romans 8:26).

My Prayer Was for a Husband

I was attending a Life in the Spirit seminar, where I was encouraged to regularly pray, read, and write. I was twenty-eight years old, lonely, and wanting to find love. Needless to say, my prayer was for a husband, and my requirements went something like this: "A Catholic man, who loves and respects his family as he will love and respect me, a man who values hard work and working together, a man who wants a family of children to raise with faith, kindness, and compassion."

Six years later after finding the fulfillment of God's love, I married my husband who was the completion of my prayer. My prayer was answered, and I now have a husband, selected for me by the Holy Spirit, and a family that I prayed for.

— *Patricia Morgetano*

WHAT IS A LIFE IN THE SPIRIT SEMINAR?

The purpose of a Life in the Spirit seminar is to introduce participants to the Holy Spirit. The sessions include prayer, music, talks, testimonies, and small-group sharing on a variety of topics such as God's love, developing a relationship with Jesus Christ, recognizing the power of the Holy Spirit, using the gifts of the Spirit, rejecting sin, growing in faith, and carrying the Good News of Jesus into the world.

"You Will Be Accepted"

Whenever my husband, Jack, and I did volunteer work, it was always social work — beginning with migrant ministry. Jack reached a point where he no longer wanted to work in the family business. He wanted to do people work. So he applied to the School of Social Work at the University of Buffalo … but something went wrong. The person in charge of the admissions committee would not even talk to Jack!

That August, we went on a family retreat vacation. We prayed our hearts out for Jack to be accepted. On our last day, one of the other mothers had a medical emergency, and our friend Mary suggested that we go into the chapel and say a pray for her. So four of us — Mary, her husband, Jack, and I — knelt to pray. We had our arms around each other. Just before Mary started to pray in tongues, I said, "Let's pray for Jack, too." So we prayed, and I had tears running from my eyes like faucets.

Later that afternoon, I said to Jack, "I'm not sure how this will work — whether it is this September or next September — but you will be accepted at the University of Buffalo. I know it is going to happen!" A few days later, we got a call from the university. The man who refused to speak to Jack took a job in California, and the woman who took his place said, "I can't understand why you were not accepted into the program. I am going to ask if I can boost you up on the list."

On September 12, the woman from the university called again. "Can your husband come in tomorrow to start school?" she asked. "He is accepted."

It was truly an answer to prayer.

— *F. de Sales Kellick*

WHAT IS PRAYING IN TONGUES?

Praying in tongues is a charism of the Holy Spirit that enables someone to pray in a language that had never been learned by that person, or that may not be a known language at all. Saint Paul described the gift of tongues in his first letter to the Corinthians as a means of speaking directly to God: "For one who speaks in a tongue speaks not to men but to God; for no one understands him, but he utters mysteries in the Spirit" (1 Corinthians 14:2). Many people say the gift of praying in tongues is a form of praise that carries them beyond the experience of reciting prayers or speaking to God in their own words.

The Gift of Calm

I was the principal of a Catholic school. It was the last day before Christmas break, and a special Mass was planned. I was surprised when the priest who had been scheduled sent a substitute instead. It was a priest I had never met before. I explained to him that I would stay for Mass, but that I had to leave immediately afterward because my mother was ill.

My mother was not the type to complain. The day before she had abdominal pain, no appetite, and was vomiting. I visited her, and we both thought she probably had a stomach flu. By evening she was very ill but refused to let us take her to the hospital.

The next morning, just before the priest arrived, I had talked to my mother and sister-in-law. Together we decided that my sister-in-law would take my mother to the hospital emergency room. I would meet them after Mass.

At the beginning of Mass, I introduced the priest to the students. During the prayers of the faithful, I was stunned when the priest announced that my mother was ill. He explained that he was a healing priest, and he asked me to come forward so that he could pray for my mother, my family, and me. I walked up to the altar. I had never been prayed over before, and I didn't know what to expect. The priest put his hands on my head and began to pray. I felt an indescribable feeling of calm come over me. I remember thinking that this must be the Holy Spirit and my mother was going to be okay.

I left for the hospital as soon as Mass ended. After many tests, the doctors determined that my mother had a ruptured bowel caused by an obstruction, but they could not take her to surgery until they regulated her blood and heart. Without the surgery she would die, but there was also a question as to whether her heart was strong enough to withstand surgery.

My dad, my brother, my husband, my children, and their spouses came at once. Each family member had a chance to talk with my mother privately. A priest, who is a family friend, gave my mother the sacrament of the sick. She was ready for surgery.

Our family was gathered in the surgical waiting room when we heard the "Code Blue" announcement over the intercom. I knew immediately that it was for my mother. A short time later, the doctor told us that her heart had stopped and they revived her, but that it was impossible to continue with the surgery. They brought her back to the hospital room where we all gathered at her bedside. The doctor explained that she would not be able to speak, but that she would be able to hear us if we wanted to say good-bye. We were with her when she took her last breath. All I could think of was to comfort my father, brother, sister-in-law, and children.

The next day, overwhelming waves of grief consumed me. A deacon, who is a friend of the family and had been at the hospital with us the day before, stopped by the house to see how I was doing. I was surprised when he commented on how calm and strong I had been the day before. It was then that I realized the Holy Spirit had not come to heal my mother, but to instill in me a sense of calm and to sustain me during one of the most difficult days of my life.

— *Rose Mary Buscaglia*

WHAT IS A HEALING PRIEST?

Technically, there is no such thing as a *healing* priest because only God can heal. But the *Catechism of the Catholic Church* recognizes that the Holy Spirit has given to some priests, religious, and lay people a special charism of healing "so as to make manifest the power of the grace of the risen Lord." Frequently, these healing ministries take place within the celebration of the Mass or during a prayer service.

"Carry Me Forth"

During the 2006 Pikes Peak Ascent Race, I had a personal goal of breaking three hours, which is typically accomplished by only 50 of the 2,000 runners. The top of the mountain was fogged in on the day of the race, so I didn't have any references for my pace. At 2 hours and 50 minutes into the race, I asked God to guide me to the top, and I surrendered my three-hour goal to him for his glory.

Five minutes later, I could hear the crowd. I let God know that if it was his will, I would do my part to break three hours, and if I did, I would shout his glory from the top of the mountain. With one minute to go, I could finally see the finish line through the fog, but I knew I could not reach it on my own power. I said my third prayer: "Come, Holy Spirit, carry me forth."

I don't remember that final minute. I don't remember touching the ground. I felt like I was walking on a cloud. Onlookers said I raced over the boulders to the top, which really surprised the crowd and caused great cheering.

At the finish line, I shouted with joy, and then I collapsed. My time was 2 hours, 59 minutes, and 51 seconds. I had reached the top with nine seconds to spare. A newspaper reporter wrote that it was the most exciting finish of the day.

— *Pat Castle*

NATIONAL LIFE RUNNERS TEAM

After the Pikes Peak Ascent Race, Pat Castle and his friend Rich Reich became the co-founders of the National LIFE Runners Team, which started with a dozen runners who wanted to join their love of running with prayers to end abortion. National LIFE Runners has grown to over 4,500 runners and walkers from ages one to one hundred one in all fifty states and twenty-seven countries.

CHAPTER 4

"If Today You Hear His Voice ..."

Throughout Scripture, we see many different examples of God speaking to people. As Catholics, we are also familiar with stories from the lives of saints to whom God has spoken. Some people wonder if God still speaks to us today.

The answer is yes. God does speak to us, and the way in which God speaks is always personal and unique.

For some, it may be a mystical experience in which they hear the voice of God actually speaking aloud. For others, it is a deep interior voice that is not audible but is still very real. God sometimes uses nature, a personal crisis, or ordinary experiences as a vehicle for speaking to us. God also uses other people as instruments in communicating with us.

It is not uncommon for God to speak to us through the words of Scripture. Reading a passage slowly, allowing the message to sink into our hearts, and then reflecting on what God is trying to tell us is a powerful way to hear what God is saying. The Lord also speaks through liturgy — the music, the readings, the homily, the prayers of the Mass, and during our own Communion meditation. It's not unusual for different people, who were all present at Mass together, to come away with very individual messages from God.

The key to hearing God's voice is to be open to receiving God's word. Most Catholics are familiar with responsorial Psalm

95, which urges, "If today you hear his voice, harden not your hearts."

Pope Francis suggests that we pray the powerful words that Eli recommended to Samuel when it became clear that the Lord was calling Samuel in the night: "Speak, LORD, because your servant is listening" (see 1 Samuel 3:1–10). "We should pray this many times a day," Pope Francis advises, "when we have a doubt, when we do not know what to do, or when we want simply to pray."

The stories in this chapter illustrate some of the different ways people have heard the deep interior voice of God in answer to their prayers, and how these people responded to God's message.

"I Shall Work Through You"

A good friend of mine called one day to ask if I would assist her with a very difficult task. Two children living in our area had both been born without an outer layer of skin on three-fourths of their bodies. They had to be bandaged daily because of a bloody discharge. The bandages had to be covered with Vaseline before they could be applied to the oozing tissue.

I reminded my friend of my lack of nursing skills, my susceptibility to odors, and my weakness in observing open sores, but she still felt I was the one to help in this work of mercy. As the day drew closer for us to go to the home of these special souls, my courage began to fade. I found myself waking at night in prayer, only to be reassured over and over again that, "Yes, Nancy, I shall be with you, and I shall work through you."

The Lord did support us. I prayed as we went about our work applying the bandages. But my prayer was one of thanksgiving to God for allowing me the privilege of performing the hardest task of my entire life. The beauty of those deformed, bleeding souls was beyond anything I have ever experienced. The strength of God allowed me to go back another day and apply the bandages myself. Compassion and love filled my being. Jesus took away my pounding headache and my shaky knees.

— *Nancy Allaire Donohue*

TRUSTING GOD

When faced with something that we know is beyond our human capabilities, we often find ourselves filled with fear and worry. It is in these anxiety-filled moments that we are called to trust God. The words of Isaiah remind us that trust in God will carry us through whatever difficulties we face in our lives:

> Have you not known? Have you not heard?
> The LORD is the everlasting God,
> the Creator of the ends of the earth.
> He does not faint or grow weary,
> his understanding is unsearchable.
> He gives power to the faint,
> and to him who has no might he increases
> strength. (Isaiah 40:28–29)

GOD WAS DIRECTING ME

Nearly two decades ago, my wife, Mary Lou, was hired to work at the circulation desk at the public library. At the end of her first week, she had lost her key to the library. This was no small matter. In the wrong hands, the key could open the door for the theft of hundreds of valuable books, audios, and videos. Re-keying the library would cost hundreds of dollars and may have cost Mary Lou her job.

We prayed intently for the Lord to help us find the key. We even used my mother's handy prayer that always seemed to work: "Jesus, lost and found, help us to find what we've lost."

Over the weekend, we searched everywhere. We dumped Mary Lou's purses and briefcases. We scoured the van and the car. We raked through the lawn near the driveway. We ransacked the house. No key.

On Monday morning, Mary Lou decided with fear and trembling that she would have to report the lost key to her supervisor.

"This cannot happen, Lord," I prayed. "Let me find that key now." At that moment, I felt as if God was telling me to check the van one more time. Since we had already searched there many times, it did not seem promising. But when I looked under the driver's seat, the key was right there in plain sight!

How had that happened? Had we simply not seen it before? Had one of our children played a silly prank, wised up, and put it where we would find it? Or did the Lord find it and put it there because he loved Mary Lou? No matter which option, we thanked God for a little miraculous answer to our prayer.

— *Bert Ghezzi*

"Where Is a Loving God?"

At age eighteen, I went away to nursing school. I loved it. I could bring smiles to sad faces, take people's pain away, and make them more comfortable. I was good at taking care of people.

But then, as part of my education, I had to go to a mental hospital for three months. It became a torture chamber for me. All I could see was hopelessness in these suffering people. Their mental afflictions seemed worse than any physical suffering I had experienced. My heart cried out, "Where is there a loving

God with all this human suffering?" Darkness of the soul began to enfold me like claws in the night.

After I returned to a medical floor at the hospital, one of the first patients assigned to me was a young woman with three small daughters. Her husband had abandoned her. This young woman was so courageous, but she lost her battle to cancer, and she died. Again my heart cried out, "Where is a loving God with all this human suffering?"

I had been raised a Methodist, and I had cherished my faith since I was a little girl. It had always brought me comfort. But now my faith was dying. I called the minister at my church and he told me, "Don't worry. Everyone goes through disbelief at one time or another."

I felt completely empty and afraid. Then I heard the voice of God for the first time in my life say, "Go to the cathedral." I knew this voice did not come from me because I had always been warned about Catholics. But I was desperate. With shaking legs and a pounding heart, I went to the Catholic cathedral.

A priest opened the door.

"I'm a Protestant," I said.

He invited me to come in, and he listened to my story with tears running down his face. He shared the time in his life when he felt this same terrible darkness. He knew my heart. He promised me that if I would seek God with all my heart, Jesus would reveal himself to me in ways I could never dream, and nothing would ever take my faith away again.

I felt as if I had been wrapped in a mantle of peace. He gave me his blessing, and I left with hope in my heart. I continued to meet with him for the next few months, and eventually I became a Catholic. The voice of God led me to the Catholic Church and a new life.

— *Kathleen Skipper*

DEALING WITH DOUBTS

Doubts can make us feel as if we have lost our faith. But doubts are not always a bad thing. When we struggle with doubts, it means we don't have enough information to resolve whatever is troubling us. Our doubts prompt us to start looking for answers. We begin to seek out people who can help us grasp whatever it is that we don't understand.

"Of course, everyone has doubts at times!" Pope Francis explains. "Doubts which touch the faith, in a positive way, are a sign that we want to know better and more fully God, Jesus, and the mystery of his love for us.... These are doubts which bring about growth! It is good, therefore, that we ask questions about our faith, because in this way we are pushed to deepen it."

"Speak to Me, Child"

When I was thirty years old, I was diagnosed with breast cancer. I went through surgery, chemo, and radiation. Afterward, I was fine. My husband and I always wanted children, but my body had been through a lot, and my chances of getting pregnant were slim. I prayed, "God, whatever is meant to be, it will happen. This is in your hands."

We were living in Switzerland at the time. Almost ten years later, my husband was offered a job in Canada, where I grew up. Six weeks after we moved to Canada, I found out I was pregnant at age forty. This pregnancy was a miracle. Benjamin was born healthy — a happy, smiley baby.

When Benjamin was twelve weeks old, the cancer came back in my liver, bones, and lungs. My family and friends were devastated, but I said, "Nope. God is going to take care of me." I told the doctors that I would do everything they told me to do, but I did not want to hear any details about the cancer, and I did not want to know the prognosis. I didn't want their voices in my head. I prayed, "God, I am your child. Sickness is not supposed to be part of our lives. You died on the cross to save us. I am giving all of this to you."

I was raised Catholic, and prayer has always been a part of my life. A healing priest told me that in my prayer, I should thank God for healing me. He said physical healing is not the only way God heals. Emotional stability is an important part of healing. So my prayers became prayers of thanksgiving for the way God was working in my life. I decided to live as if I was already healed.

Things went really well for the first few months, but then it got ugly again. I had pain in my back and hip. They tried radiation and more chemo. Then I got pneumonia. I could not get out of bed. I lost weight, and I was completely out of it because of the painkillers. I couldn't hold my baby for weeks. My family thought this was the end. But suddenly, I heard a voice say, "Speak to me, child."

A profound sense of childlike faith and belief came over me. I prayed out loud, "Lord, I believe I am supposed to be here for my child and my husband, and as a testimony to you. If this is supposed to be, I know you will make it happen. But if you are going to take me, then please just do it."

I went to sleep, and the next morning I woke up with no fever and a lot of energy. I got out of bed and began to take care of Benjamin. I also gained a new understanding of childlike faith. When my son needs something, I take care of him. God was taking care of me in the same way.

There were several more good months, but then the chemo stopped working. I asked about an experimental drug. It would be risky because I would have to be off chemo for four weeks before I could start the battery of tests to see if I would qualify for the clinical trial. I prayed about it, and I had the feeling that this was something I needed to do.

Four weeks later, I passed all of the tests except the last one. My hemoglobin level needed to reach 90. It was 83. I begged the nurse to give me twenty-four hours and let me try again. A lot of people and prayer groups were praying for me, so I went home and sent messages to everyone to pray. I ate foods that would boost the iron in my blood. When I went back the next day, my hemoglobin was 90.

This was a randomized clinical trial, so the next hurdle was to find out if I would receive the experimental drug or regular chemo. I prayed, "God, it is up to you whether this is the right drug for me. I give it to you to decide what is for my greatest good." Later that afternoon, I was told I would receive the experimental drug.

The drug started working immediately. My health is now stable. Lumps in my bones disappeared. My scans show tumors shrinking. I haven't been sick. I am living a totally normal life with a lot of energy, and I am able to take care of my son.

Throughout all of this, I learned that it's not just about praying. It's also about believing. It's about giving everything to God and putting yourself into a state of receivership. It's about having a childlike faith that God will take care of you no matter what happens.

— *Maria Eisenring*

THE BEAUTY OF CHILDLIKE FAITH

"A child has nothing to give and everything to receive," Pope Francis explains. "A child is vulnerable, and depends on his or her father and mother. The one who becomes like a little child is poor in self but rich in God. Children, who have no problem in understanding God, have much to teach us: they tell us that he accomplishes great things in those who put up no resistance to him, who are simple and sincere, without duplicity."

"Be Still"

I taught school for forty-seven years, and everything I did had to do with teaching. I enjoyed teaching, but after forty-seven years I said to myself, "It's time to move on!"

I had no idea what I would do. I was offered a few different positions, but they did not seem like a good fit. I started going out for prayer walks. It was winter, and one day I stopped by a dormant tree. I saw this tree as a symbol of strength because it held the promise of new life in the spring. Then I heard an interior voice saying, "Be still."

I opened my hands and my heart, and I prayed, "Help me to let go. I give you my life. I need a new view. Show me the way."

A few weeks later, I received a call from a woman who invited me to lunch. She offered me a position in a medical office. I had no knowledge of taking a temperature or a blood pressure. I said, "There is no way I could accept this position."

She said, "Why don't you come in tomorrow and check it out?"

So the next day I went to the medical office, and I shadowed someone all day. I went back the next day, and three years later, I was still working there. For the first year and a half, I took temperatures and blood pressures when the patients came in. I learned how to do EKGs and breathing treatments. I truly enjoyed this new ministry.

Then I was asked to move into the office, where I would be doing clerical work and making follow-up appointments. At first, I didn't think I wanted to move because I loved the connection that I had with the patients. But now the patients come to me after they leave the doctor, and I can be a life-giving presence to those who are sick or suffering.

If they need surgery, I give them a medal and say, "Keep this." Or I hand them a little heart and say, "I will hold you in my heart." At times, I present patients with a prayer shawl and pray with them.

This job was truly an answer to prayer. It has transformed my life and lifted my faith in God to new heights. I will always have an attitude of gratitude for this experience.

— *Sister Barbara Whelan, O.S.F.*

WHAT IS A PRAYER WALK?

A prayer walk is simply praying while walking. Some people prefer prayer walking in the countryside, on a beach, or in a park because the beauty of nature lifts one's heart and mind to God. But prayer walks can take place in the neighborhood, on a treadmill, in a shopping mall, on the way to work, or in any place where you want to transform walking into a form of prayer.

"I Kept My Promise"

I was twenty-seven years old when I divorced a very abusive, violent, vindictive man, who had discovered the best way to hurt me was by abusing our four children. Once we were divorced, he continued to abuse and harass us. Somewhere along the way, I became fearful that he would actually succeed in killing me. I was obsessed with the thought that if I died, he would fight my parents for custody of the children — not because he loved and cared about his children, but to hurt everyone.

So I prayed (*begged* is probably a better word) and asked God to let me live long enough to see my children grow up, and be happy, and able to take care of themselves. After a few weeks of asking for this favor over and over, I decided God had gotten the message. I calmed down, let it go, and actually forgot about it.

Years later, I got a phone call from my daughter-in-law telling me my thirty-two-year-old son, Thom, had a massive heart attack at work and died. Before I could react or even say a word, I very clearly heard a voice say, "I kept my promise." I instantly knew it was the voice of God. The grace and mercy of those words enabled me to accept Thom's death and to be there for my other children.

A few years later, my son, Michael, had an extreme flare-up of a rare enzyme deficiency disease that he had since childhood. His body was shutting down, and the doctors thought he might not survive. I could not bear the thought of losing another child. I begged for God not to take my son, but I also told God I would not be mad if he took Michael home. I asked only that He give Mike a happy death if that was his will.

I immediately felt God's grace flow into me. I felt peaceful. I knew I had done the correct thing even though it was so difficult to think of what might happen. A couple of hours later Mike's wife called to say he was on the mend, and he hasn't had another flare-up like that since.

— *Susan Stout*

CHAPTER 5

Signs from Above

There are times when something supernatural breaks through our ordinary existence. We may become aware of God's presence, or we may feel as if Our Lady, the saints, or angels are near. We may feel as if we have received a sign from above.

These kinds of mystical experiences are not common, but they are also not rare. According to a Pew Forum survey, 37 percent of Catholics reported that they have had a mystical experience at some point in their lives. These experiences involved a vision, an unexplained coincidence, or some spiritual happening that went beyond the ordinary and left a lasting impression.

Mystical experiences are not something that people can conjure up on their own. These kinds of experiences tend to happen unexpectedly and are so profound that they are often difficult for people to describe adequately.

Most of these experiences take place in an instant, which leaves the person feeling as if he or she has crossed over into some spiritual realm. The result is almost always some new insight, awareness, knowledge, or truth. Sometimes, the experience offers consolation and encouragement. Other times it instills in the person a feeling of courage and a renewed sense of zeal. It almost always leaves the person with feelings of deep reverence and awe.

Pope Francis acknowledged that he rarely has mystical experiences, but there was one experience of God's loving presence that had a profound impact on him. It happened in 1953 on the feast of Saint Matthew. Seventeen-year-old Jorge Bergoglio had just gone to confession when "he felt his heart touched and he sensed the descent of the Mercy of God, who with a gaze of tender love, called him to religious life."

We have no way of knowing why some people have these kinds of supernatural experiences and others do not. It is part of the great mystery of God, who knows each of us intimately and interacts with us in ways that we may not understand. Whether or not we ever have a mystical experience, we can trust that God is constantly pursuing us with the hope of drawing us more closely to himself.

In this chapter, we see stories of people who have experienced a supernatural event that made a deep spiritual impact on them and changed their lives forever.

"I Don't Know Where I Am!"

I was working as a welder, and my boss wanted to send me on a job out of town. Another guy was supposed to go with me because I have no sense of direction, but he messed up a job, and he had to stay back and fix it. My boss told me I would have to go by myself. I remember standing in the shop and praying, "Lord, I have to go. I'll trust in you."

I got my tools together, and as I was running out the door, I banged my head and cut myself wide open. They sent me over to the hospital. I prayed, "Okay, Lord, is this a sign not to go or what?"

Well, the doctor at the hospital stitched me up, and I got to the airport on time. The flight was scheduled to land at 3:00 in the afternoon, and I thought that would be great because I would be able to find my way in the daylight. But then the airline announced the flight was delayed. I prayed, "Okay, Lord, I'm getting nervous. But I am supposed to trust that you will get me through this." I could feel myself sweating.

Finally, they got us on the plane, and we were supposed to take off, but they announced that there were mechanical problems. We were going to have to switch planes. I was a nervous wreck, and I prayed, "Okay, Lord, I am not going to walk out into the parking lot and go home. I am going to trust you."

Finally, we got on a flight, and we landed in Greensboro, North Carolina, at 11:30 at night. I picked up a rental car, and they gave me directions. I drove out of the airport, and I ended up in the middle of nowhere. It was pitch black. I prayed, "Lord, I need you now more than ever. I can't do this. I don't know where I am!"

When I looked up, I saw a faint light in the distance, and I thought that maybe it was a house. It looked like an old chicken coop. I pulled the car up to it, and I started to get out of the car, but all of a sudden, a girl came out of nowhere. She was barefoot. I told her I was lost. She said, "I know where you are going. Stay on this road and count eleven stoplights. Then make a right and you'll be there."

I couldn't even say thank you and she was gone.

I prayed, "Okay, Lord, I am going to do what she said." I counted eleven lights, made a right, and I was in the parking lot of the hotel. I don't know if she was an angel, but she was definitely an answer to prayer. I got to the job the next day, and it all worked out.

— *Mark Piscitello*

WHAT CATHOLICS BELIEVE ABOUT ANGELS

According to the *Catechism of the Catholic Church*, angels are "*servants* and messengers of God." They are spiritual creatures with intelligence and a free will. Catholics believe that we benefit from the mysterious and powerful assistance of angels — especially our guardian angel. Throughout our lives we are surrounded by our guardian angel's watchful protection and intercession.

My Guardian Angel

I had come home from the hospital after a total hysterectomy, when I started having severe pains in my abdomen. My husband called the doctor who said, "Bring her back to the hospital immediately."

They suspected that I had developed an obstructed bowel from the anesthesia. The decision was made to wait and see if it would fix itself. In the meantime, I was in excruciating pain. They were giving me pain killers, but it didn't help.

I had two little girls at the time — ages fourteen and eleven. I never thought I would put anything ahead of my daughters, but the pain was so awful that I just didn't want to live any longer. I prayed, "Oh, dear God, please take me. I just can't bear this any longer."

In the middle of the night, my hospital room door was open, and there was light coming in from the hallway. I felt weight at the end of my bed near my feet. So I opened my eyes, and my guardian angel was there. It was a unisex person with a bowl-type haircut and clothes like a monk would wear. I could not see facial features because the room was dark.

Without speaking any words, she said to me, "You're going to be okay. Don't worry." And she patted my leg. I closed my eyes and went to sleep.

I had no more pain after that. The next day I told my husband what happened and he said, "You were pumped up with so many drugs that you were hallucinating." But I never believed that for a minute. It happened in 1990, and I can still feel it. It is like something that happened yesterday.

A friend of mine told me that when you get messages from angels they don't directly speak to you. It's a form of telepathy. You hear what they are saying, but it's not how we communicate back and forth here on earth.

I feel really blessed that I had that visit. It has changed my whole way of praying. Now I don't ever ask for something. I pray for God's will, or if I am praying for someone who is sick, I ask that they will be given the strength to go through it. I never look beyond the things I already have. I try to focus on people who don't have as much as I do.

— *Lina D'Amore*

PRAYER TO OUR GUARDIAN ANGEL

Angel of God, my guardian dear, to whom God's love commits me here, ever this day be at my side, to light and guard, to rule and guide. Amen.

Let Nothing Disturb You

I was at home praying for a sign that everything was going to be okay and asking for additional help from Saint Teresa of Ávila. That evening, I was scheduled to take part in a live, half-hour talk show on local television with a gay-rights activist and a Catholic lawyer. The topic was religious freedom and gay rights. I felt a wave of fear come over me. Why had I said yes to this?

Under normal circumstances I would not be afraid. As a broadcast journalist for thirty years, I was accustomed to doing secular interviews on faith-based topics, but this invitation came after I had endured a hostile on-air exchange with a reporter from that station a few days before. Now I was being given another chance to inject truth into the distortion of the first interview.

I paced the floor thinking, "What if this is a setup?"

Ashamed and embarrassed by my weakness, I prayed out loud, "Saint Teresa, please help me."

Within seconds, I heard the mailman on the porch. He brought a package from a radio listener of mine. When I opened the box, I saw a card with the words, "Let nothing disturb you: Teresa of Ávila." Under the wrapping paper, there was a lovely bronze statue of Saint Teresa of Ávila.

I started laughing and crying at the same time. Needless to say, the interview went well.

— *Teresa Tomeo*

PRAYER OF SAINT TERESA OF ÁVILA

Let nothing disturb you.
Let nothing frighten you.
All things are passing away.
God never changes.
Patience obtains all things.
Whoever has God lacks nothing;
God alone suffices.

A Ray of Sunlight

When my husband, Kirk, and I first met, he was a devout Catholic. For years we attended daily Mass together. Then with the changes in the Church after the Second Vatican Council (1961–

1965), his brilliant mind started questioning, and he stopped believing. He was still a Christian in his actions — a kind, loving, giving person — but he didn't believe.

One day, Kirk drove me to the hospital where I needed to have routine blood work done. There were quite a few people in line for blood work, so Kirk decided to wait outside on a bench in a little memorial garden. Kirk had recently been diagnosed with peritoneal mesothelioma. When I came out of the hospital, Kirk told me he had been sitting there and asked God if he should return to the Church. It was a dark, cloudy day. He said that as he talked to God, there was an opening in the clouds and a ray of sunlight hit his abdomen.

Later that day, Kirk called a priest and went to confession. From then on, he attended Mass daily.

Kirk's return to the Church was a special gift to him. His renewed belief in God kept him going through surgery, chemo trials, and abdominal draining. Many of the wonderful people we met at the trials died within a year, but Kirk kept on going. Until the end, he always believed that he would be healed.

Kirk's return to the Church was a special gift to me, too, because his renewed belief in God always made him positive. Living away from home for different clinical trials became adventures instead of sad times. We found many nice churches and met many nice people. Kirk died at home after a three-and-a-half-year battle with cancer.

— *Pat Webster*

A Good Friday Miracle

Every year on Good Friday, Pro-Life Wisconsin prays the Stations of the Cross at St. Rita's Catholic Church, and then we process solemnly to pray at a nearby abortion facility. The event always draws a big crowd.

On April 22, 2011, we had about 125 people praying at the clinic for an end to abortion. We had almost finished our prayers when a young man came out of the crowd and asked if we could pray the Chaplet of the Holy Face of Jesus. He promised that it wouldn't take more than seven minutes. I asked him to lead the prayer — and he did.

Just before we wrapped things up, I noticed a lot of police in the area. They weren't there because of us. They were directing traffic because the signals had lost power. Then, I noticed the neon sign in the clinic window was not glowing, and neither were the lights in the store next door. Suddenly, clinic employees started exiting the building. Their electrical power had been cut, and they were hurrying to their cars to grab flashlights. After that, a wave of women came streaming out of the clinic.

Realizing that we just weren't going to get an opportunity to talk with each of these women individually, I called out, "Go home to enjoy Easter for what it really is — NEW LIFE! Don't come back! This is a sign from God! Today is Good Friday — the day our Lord and Savior died on the cross for our sins!"

Some of the women kept walking, but others turned around. Some even smiled at me!

After everything settled down, I remained at the clinic with a friend, talking, praying, and taking in all that had happened. My friend looked across the street at the Pro-Life Women's Care Center. Their lights were on, but all the other lights in the area were still out.

Typical me — the doubter — I checked with the Women's Care Center to see if they had a generator or any other way to produce electricity. They said no. Someone else did some checking and found out that the Women's Care Center was on the same grid as the other homes and businesses. The utility company said it would be impossible for them to have electricity when the grid was out. But their lights were on!

No one knows why the Pro-Life Women's Care Center was the only place that had electricity that afternoon. No one knows what happened to the young man who encouraged us to pray the Chaplet to the Holy Face of Jesus that day. No one knows if any babies were saved from abortion that day. But my heart tells me all of this was more than an answer to prayer. It was a Good Friday miracle.

— *Dan Miller*

THE CHAPLET OF THE HOLY FACE

This prayer calls to mind the five senses of Christ — sight, hearing, smell, taste, and touch — during the Crucifixion. The chaplet is prayed on a special set of prayer beads, with six large beads, representing Christ's face and his five senses, and thirty-three small beads, representing his thirty-three years on earth.

To pray the chaplet, make the Sign of the Cross and pray: "O God, incline unto my aid. O Lord, make haste to help me."

On the first large bead, reflect on the face of Christ. This bead is followed by three small beads representing Jesus' three years of public ministry.

Each of the remaining five large beads are followed by six small beads. On each of the five large beads, reflect on one of the five senses of Jesus and pray the Glory Be followed by the words, "My Jesus, mercy."

On the small beads pray, "Arise, O Lord, and let thy enemies be scattered, and let them that hate thee flee before thy face."

At the end, pray the Glory Be seven times in memory of the last seven words that Jesus spoke on the cross and the seven sorrows of Our Lady.

Conclude with the prayer: "O God, our Protector, look down upon us and cast thine eyes upon the Face of Christ."

It Is God Who Cures

I had a serious cancer tumor inside my nose, but I had every confidence that my Our Fathers and Hail Marys would ensure that the surgery would be done satisfactorily. Three days after the surgery, the doctor checked me over, and he ever so humbly said, "By the way, I got it all."

Both of us were so happy, we grabbed each other's hand for a strong shake while looking directly into each other's eyes. And then, something quite unusual happened. The doctor's face transformed itself into one huge host. When our hands released, I saw just my surgeon's happy face again.

Surely, God had been reminding me, "It is I who cure."

And so that afternoon I was literally prancing over the sidewalks. To this day, my heart still beats with extra love and thanks for God's holy presence and care.

— *Elizabeth Fenn*

Mark's Blessed Mother

Ten years after my last child was born, I discovered at age thirty-nine that I was pregnant. I was ecstatic. During my pregnancy, my husband and I dedicated our unborn child to the Blessed Mother.

Mark James came merrily into our lives at a hefty 9 pounds and 4 ounces. Our pediatrician assured us that he was perfect. But at age three, Mark was diagnosed with stage four Wilms' tumor, a rare childhood cancer that starts in the kidneys. The only prayer I could utter was, "Help!"

Mark endured three major surgeries, two minor surgeries, two rounds of radiation, and two and a half years of torturous chemotherapy.

One day, after a radiation treatment, my three-year-old son came back to the waiting room and told me that he saw the Blessed Mother on the wall. I am ashamed to say that I didn't even know that he knew who the Blessed Mother was. We were in a public hospital. There couldn't be any statues on the wall. But Mark insisted that the Blessed Mother was on the wall.

The next day he came back from radiation and said, "I saw her again!" I asked what she looked like. He said she was beautiful with long, brown hair. She had a blue robe and a white towel on her head. I asked if she said anything, and he replied, "Oh, yes! She said, 'Mark, I love you, and you are being healed!' "

I was speechless. How could a three-year-old with virtually no knowledge of the Blessed Mother make up such a story? I wanted to believe. I asked the Blessed Mother for a sign, and as we descended down the stairs to the main floor, I was overcome with the scent of roses. I almost fainted.

Mark's relationship with Our Lady continued. He wanted a statue of the Blessed Mother. When his grandmother brought him a statue of Our Lady of Victory, he told her, "That's a nice Blessed Mother, Grandma, but it isn't my Blessed Mother." When I took him to a shrine of Our Lady of Fátima, he thought this Blessed Mother was also very beautiful, but it was not "his" Blessed Mother. Finally, someone gave him a small, plastic statue of Our Lady of Grace — blue robe, white towel over her head, dark brown hair. This was his Blessed Mother, and she became his constant companion.

But where was the healing that Mark's Blessed Mother had promised? His cancer would be gone for a while, and then return with a vengeance. Throughout all of this, Mark demonstrated trust, gentleness, love, patience, and quiet suffering.

The morning before his last surgery, a wonderful priest asked Mark if he would like to receive Jesus. Mark led us in prayer as he received his first Holy Communion. We all had tears in our eyes, and I knew it was the presence of God that held me up.

After Mark's surgery, we received a fully-paid vacation to Florida from the Make-A-Wish Foundation. Early one morning I walked to the beach. I knew in my heart that we would be taking Mark home to die. I heard the words, "Trust me with all your heart and rely not on your own understanding." I knew it was God speaking. I had to trust.

Two months later I felt another mass in Mark's abdomen. We had Mark for six more weeks. One day, shortly before the end, Mark said, "Don't worry about me. Where I am going is beautiful!"

On September 8, a feast of the Blessed Mother, I held Mark in my arms. His final words were, "Mommy, I love you." Then he put his head on my shoulder and died in my arms. Mark was not cured from cancer. He was healed into new life.

Even though I knew death was coming, I was not prepared for its suddenness. I bathed him for the last time, mostly with my tears. I put clean pajamas on him. His face had been transformed. He looked peaceful and had a smile on his face as if he was seeing his Blessed Mother.

— *Kathleen Skipper*

A Sign That Mom Is Okay

Several years ago my independent, healthy, ninety-two-year-old mother had a dizzy spell that turned out to be more than a spell. Mom had a brain tumor, and within three and a half months, she was gone.

To say my life was shattered is putting it mildly. Mom was my best friend. All I wanted was to know for sure she was safe. That became my prayer: "Please, Lord, give me a sign that Mom is okay."

Six months after I started praying for a sign, I was making my annual novena to the Infant of Prague in my childhood church with five close friends. I asked the Infant of Prague to send me a sign. Monday night and Tuesday night were routine. On Wednesday night, we took our regular seats, and no one sat in the pew in front of us. Right after Communion, the friend next to me reached for something on the seat in front of her. It was the size of a Chinese fortune cookie message. After she looked at it, she turned to me and said, "I think this is for you."

It was an address label from an apartment my mother had moved into after my dad passed away. My mother had left that apartment fourteen years before she died, and we didn't have any of those address labels anymore. I was so stunned and so excited. I finally had my sign! No one could explain how that label showed up in the pew in front of me from an apartment Mom had not lived in for fourteen years. It was a true miracle. And I am sure Mom got a kick out of watching me tell my husband, my sons, my brother and two sisters, and anyone who would listen about my sign. I carry the label in my purse all the time. When someone needs a little faith push, I tell my story.

— *Sandy Zambotti*

CHAPTER 6

I Need a Miracle!

Some people will tell you miracles happen all the time. They attribute miracle status to anything good that occurs. "It was a miracle that I got to work in all that traffic.... It was a miracle that our team won the championship.... It was a miracle that I didn't get caught in the storm!"

Other people will tell you there is no such thing as a miracle. "There is an explanation for everything.... Today's miracle will be tomorrow's scientific breakthrough.... A miracle is just a coincidence or a twist of fate."

The truth about miracles lies between these two extremes.

Catholics believe that miracles happen, but they are not commonplace. A miracle occurs when God intervenes in the course of nature and allows something to happen that defies scientific explanation. The result is always something good. In fact, the Church requires documented miracles in the beatification and canonization process. The miracle must be the result of prayer to a holy person who is being considered for sainthood.

Pope Francis tells us that in praying for a miracle, we must pray with courage, humility, and strong faith. He tells the story of a little girl in Argentina, who was only given a few hours to live. Her father took a bus to the Marian Shrine at Luján, about seventy kilometers away, but arrived after the shrine had closed. "And he began to pray to Our Lady with his hands gripping the iron fence. And he prayed, and prayed, and wept, and prayed … and that's the way he remained all night long." When the man returned home the next morning, his wife told him their daughter's fever broke, and that she was going to be all right. "Prayer works wonders," the pope concluded, "but we have to believe!"

In this chapter, you will find powerful stories of people who prayed for a miracle and believed that God would answer their prayer.

God Healed Me

I was in the intensive care unit with Guillain-Barré syndrome, an autoimmune disorder in which the body's immune system attacks the peripheral nervous system. I was paralyzed, and I thought I was going to die. I was terrified. But a nun from my prayer group gave me a written prophesy that said God was going to heal me, and he did. Most people who survive the paralysis suffer with the Guillain-Barré syndrome for three or four months. Then they have to deal with residual damage. I walked away in fourteen days with no damage, and I gave all of the glory and honor to God.

— *Carolyn McLean*

Your Daughter Is a Miracle

The day our family welcomed Sarah was a dramatic day. It was March 16, 2013, a date my husband and I never forget because of John 3:16. After a healthy pregnancy, normal ultrasounds, and a naturally progressive labor, everything came to a halt when Sarah's and my heart rate skyrocketed. My family doctor told me I would need a cesarean section.

I'd never undergone a major surgery. Worn and weary from having been in labor over twenty-four hours, I sobbed openly. As I wept, a spiritual darkness swept over me. It was as if a black cloud loomed over my head, and all became silent. The joy of anticipation transformed into fear and worry. Nearing despair, I had no energy for prayer, yet a tiny voice within encouraged me, "Say a prayer to Father Solanus Casey." I knew it was Divine Providence, because I wasn't even remotely thinking about Venerable Solanus Casey. Silently I prayed, "Father Solanus, please help me."

Shortly thereafter, I was wheeled into the operating room, but everything had changed. I was immersed in the "peace that surpasses all understanding," and the room itself appeared to be sublimely illuminated, but I thought that was just my imagination.

Once the on-call physician, whom I'd never met before, delivered Sarah, the room fell eerily silent.

A pediatrician inquired, "Do you have any genetic disorders in your family?"

Naively, I replied, "No. Why?"

She summoned my husband over to Sarah, and they briefly conversed. My maternal heart knew something was gravely wrong.

When I held Sarah for the first time, hours later, I wept again. She had buggy eyes, a protruding forehead, and little mitten hands. The unofficial diagnosis was a rare disease called Apert syndrome, and my husband and I didn't know if our sweet Sarah would live or die. In those hours of raw emotion and grief, the on-call physician entered my recovery room with eyes widened.

"I'll never forget delivering your daughter today," she said. "When the medical staff and I walked into the operating room with you, we all agreed that we felt a supernatural presence with us. Then, as I reached my hand into your womb to deliver Sarah, I felt God's hand take over mine. It was God's hand who delivered your daughter. God has special plans for Sarah. Even the operation itself went flawlessly, which doesn't happen. Your daughter is a miracle, one I'll never forget."

Her words were so confident that I was convinced that Venerable Solanus Casey had aided me with his intercession. That day was just the beginning of many incredible miracles surrounding Sarah's life. We call her our "medical marvel," because she has bypassed many of the typical procedures and surgeries that kids with Apert syndrome have to endure.

— Jeannie Ewing

FATHER SOLANUS CASEY, O.F.M. CAP.

Bernard Francis (Solanus) Casey (1870–1957) was a Capuchin priest who was known for his faith, humility, compassion, and ministry of spiritual and physical healing to people in New York, Detroit, and Huntington, Indiana. His cause for canonization was opened in 1982. He was declared Venerable, the first step toward sainthood, in 1995. On May 4, 2017, the Vatican announced that Pope Francis had approved a miracle attributed to Father Solanus' intercession, thus clearing the way for his beatification and his new title of Blessed, on November 18, 2017.

A Child to Love

Fourteen years ago, one of our daughters and her husband wanted a child very much. She had lost three babies before she was very far along, and was never was able to conceive again. They decided to adopt, and they had already had the regular home study done, but it looked like it would be a very long time, if ever, before they were given the blessing of a child to call their own.

I have a cousin whose family takes in foster children. At that time, they were caring for a little girl who was four years old. Our daughter had met this little girl at a family graduation party. After this visit, our daughter contacted my cousin to see if it would be possible to adopt this precious child. My cousin said the possibilities were zero to none. Our daughter wanted to pursue it, so our prayer team began to pray about this seemingly perfect but impossible placement. We needed a miracle!

Finally, the little girl was freed for adoption. The social worker decided that our daughter and her husband should come to Indiana for an interview and to spend some time with the little girl. We knew that God was in control.

The interview went well, and after that our daughter came to Indiana for a couple of months. The little girl was placed with our daughter to wait for the legal adoption. As Christmas neared, our son-in-law drove to Indiana, and they were free to take this little girl home with them. It all seemed to be going smoothly and according to God's plan.

A few days before Christmas they packed the car and started the long trip back to Florida with their precious passenger. As hard as it was to see them leave, we knew that we were in the middle of a huge blessing! They arrived home on Christmas Eve and were beyond happy! Our new granddaughter's adoption was finalized on Good Friday, and she was brought to our parish church in Indiana for baptism at the Easter Vigil!

Since they were getting older, my daughter and son-in-law were not trying to adopt anymore children, but a few years later they received a call from the same social worker telling them that a two-month-old little girl had just been surrendered.

Needless to say, they opened their hearts and home to this precious child, too. They came to Indiana the next Saturday and met their sweet baby daughter at a big family gathering! We are all thankful to God for these wonderful girls and to a caring cousin and her husband for making this all happen! God is so good!

— *Nancy Riecke*

Faith, Prayer, and Trust

On February 11, 1996, my granddaughter, Katelin Amanda McQuaid, was born. Due to her deep purple color at birth, doctors told us she had respiratory problems, and they suspected brain damage. A tracheotomy was immediately performed.

Katelin was baptized at the hospital, and she remained in neonatal intensive care for two months. She had a variety of medical issues and was not able to eat or breathe on her own. She was sent home with many unanswered questions and a very uncertain future.

Katelin required round-the-clock nursing with tubes, monitors, and medical equipment. Therapists came for early intervention, but Katelin moved from one crisis to another with multiple surgeries, and doctors still were unable to make a definitive diagnosis. By the time Katelin was twelve months old, she was still at her birth weight, and the situation was becoming desperate. I asked the Dominican and Carmelite nuns to pray for Katelin, and I had her put on many prayer chains. Katelin needed a miracle.

On Good Friday, 1997, my dad showed me a video about little Audrey Santo, who had fallen into the family pool, nearly drowned, and lapsed into a coma. Her mother took her to Medjugorje, where the family believes Audrey became a victim soul, offering her suffering for others. When Audrey returned home, there were reports of weeping statues, bleeding Communion wafers, and healings from those who visited her.

I had never experienced such things, but I believed the stories in the Bible with an open, childlike faith. On April 2, 1997, I drove into a blizzard with my daughter and Katelin to visit Audrey Santo. While there, a statue of the Blessed Mother began weeping tears, and a priest blessed Katelin with the tears coming from the statue. During the consecration at Mass, the hosts in the ciborium were covered with miraculous oil. After Mass, during Benediction, I witnessed a bleeding Host! I prayed, "My Lord and my God!"

My faith reached its fullness at that moment, and I promised God, if he healed Katelin, I would make all of this known. My prayer was answered. Katelin was healed of all her infirmities and has remained an honor student throughout her school years.

I am keeping my promise by going to daily Mass, Eucharistic Adoration, and praying the Rosary and the Divine Mercy Chaplet. I started a prayer group with six women, which has grown to over 250 prayer warriors. For almost twenty years, I have told our story and witnessed to the Real Presence of Christ in the Eucharist and the power of prayer. My family received a miracle through faith, prayer, and trust in Jesus Christ, and now I try to help others know Jesus, his mercy, and his love.

— *Dawn Curazzato*

UNDERSTANDING MEDJUGORJE

In 1981, six children reported that Our Lady had appeared to them in Medjugorje, a small town in Bosnia and Herzegovina. Three visionaries claim that Mary still appears to them daily.

Over the years, many pilgrims have traveled to Medjugorje, and some of these pilgrims claim to have experienced miraculous healings and spiritual favors.

Whenever an apparition is reported, the Church studies the claims, the messages received, and the individuals involved before determining if the apparition is "worthy of belief," or "not worthy of belief." An apparition can also be classified as "not contrary to the faith," which means there's no certainty that the apparition is authentic, but the information coming forth does not in any way conflict with Catholic beliefs.

In 2010, Pope Benedict XVI established a commission to study the reports of apparitions at Medjugorje. In 2017, Pope Francis acknowledged the spiritual and pastoral fruits that many pilgrims to Medjugorje have experienced, and he asked Archbishop Henryk Hoser of Warszawa-Praga to examine "possible pastoral initiatives for the future" at Medjugorje.

Audrey Santo

Audrey Santo was born on December 19, 1983, and died on April 14, 2007. During her life, the Church did not officially acknowledge the validity of the weeping statues and bleeding hosts. Bishop Daniel P. Reilly did remark, "The most striking evidence of the presence of God in the Santo home is seen in the dedication of the family to Audrey." After Audrey's death, a nonprofit foundation was formed for the purpose of promoting her cause for sainthood.

A Miracle Cure

When I was fifteen years old, I was diagnosed with lymphedema, an incurable disease that caused painful swelling involving the lymphatics in my legs. Over the next ten years, I had more than fifty operations. My hospitalizations lasted from one week to one year.

During my last two years of high school, I was tutored while in the hospital. Prior to developing lymphedema, I was involved in school sports, plays, or social activities. Then one day my doctors told me I could leave the hospital for a few hours to attend my prom. My mom bought me a new dress, and my boyfriend, Bob, got a leave from the Marines so he could go to the prom with me. But the evening before the prom, the doctor said, "Sorry, Maureen, but your bloodwork shows another infection. No prom."

My already weak faith became even weaker. I said, "Okay, God, what are you doing to me?" I thought I was being punished for something I had done or something I would do later in life. People told me to pray and trust God. How could I pray and trust when God kept knocking me down? I built a wall around myself and lived in my own little world of pain.

Bob would drive eighteen hours one way to visit me. Sometimes I would not talk or want to see him. I began to think this could not be true love, that Bob only felt sorry for me, so I broke up with him. I blamed God. Everything was God's fault. I found every reason not to go to Mass and confession. It was God who was wrong, not me.

Then came the day the doctor explained I would need to have my leg amputated above the knee. My loving mom, her heart heavy with pain but still a woman of great faith, would say, "God is good. He will take care of you."

My response was, "If this is good, I'd hate to see what bad is."

The amputation was difficult because I would not share my suffering with anyone. Six months after my first amputation, I needed another amputation that went up to my hip. Down came my spirits and on came depression. I knew in my heart I should turn to God, but I made myself believe that I could do it alone.

I was finally discharged and later got a job. Bob came back into my life, and this time I knew it was true love. He asked me on my birthday to marry him. Saying "yes" was the first right thing I had done in years.

Four months after the wedding, I had a miscarriage. "Okay, God, another punishment." Two years later, I became pregnant again. Our baby was born with a progressive neuromuscular disease. At twenty-one months, Bobby had his first seizure. He lost his ability to walk and talk. He was in and out of the hospital. The doctors wanted us to put him in an institution, but we refused because Bobby was the joy of our life.

During this time, my lymphedema was getting worse, and I ended up back in the hospital. My leg was so bad that I was put on an experimental pump. But the pump created serious complications. I didn't want to be bedridden for the rest of my life, and this was my only medical option.

One evening Bob went to see a movie about Sister Faustina and Divine Mercy. He tried to share it with me, but I wouldn't listen. Bob felt as if God was calling him to take our family to Poland. I tried to resist, but it was no use.

On March 23, 1981, Bobby's birthday, we arrived in Poland. On March 28, I went to confession for the first time in a long time. That night as we prayed the Chaplet of Divine Mercy at the tomb of Sister Faustina for the healing of Bobby and me, I sensed Sister Faustina say to me in my heart, "Ask for my help, and I will help you."

I said, "Okay, Faustina, I came this far from home, now do something!"

Suddenly, the pain left and the swelling in my leg was gone. I did not believe in miracles, and I was convinced that I was having a nervous breakdown. The following day as I awoke, it became clear that I had received a healing. When I returned home, I was examined by five independent doctors who came to the conclusion that I was completely healed. They had no medical explanation for the sudden healing of this incurable disease.

After the trip to Poland, Bobby received a partial healing for three and a half to four years, but then his health failed from complications due to surgery. As a result, Bobby went to the Lord in May 1991. The accumulated evidence of my miracle cure was examined in consultation by five doctors appointed by the Sacred Congregation for the Causes of Saints. Having passed this test, my case was examined by a team of theologians, and finally by a team of cardinals and bishops. My cure was accepted by all as a miracle through Sister Faustina's intercession, which resulted in her beatification.

— *Maureen Digan*

SAINT FAUSTINA KOWALSKA, APOSTLE OF DIVINE MERCY

Saint Faustina Kowalska (1905–1938) was born in Głogowiec, Poland. At age twenty, she entered the Congregation of the Sisters of Our Lady of Mercy and took the name Sister Maria Faustina of the Blessed Sacrament. Throughout her life, Sister Faustina received apparitions of Jesus, which she recorded in her diary. These apparitions formed the basis for the devotion to Divine Mercy. An artist painted an image of Jesus as Divine Mercy based on Sister Faustina's visions. Sister Faustina was canonized on April 30, 2000, by Pope John Paul II, who established the feast of Divine Mercy on the first Sunday after Easter.

Prayer to Divine Mercy

The following prayer to the Divine Mercy was written by Maureen's husband, Deacon Bob Digan.

> O Lord, our God,
> We place all our TRUST in you, because you are mercy itself.
> We repent of our sins and turn to you for mercy.

We trust you to provide for our every need, according to your will.
Help us to forgive others as you forgive us.
We promise to be merciful by our deeds, words, and prayers.
Though we have fears because of human weakness, we rely on your infinite goodness and mercy.
We entrust to your mercy our very lives, our present situation, and our uncertain future.
We entrust to you the future of our planet, our Church, our nations, our families, and all our needs.
With loud cries, we implore your mercy on us and the whole world.
Look upon us created in your image and likeness.
Form us in the Heart of Mary, by the power of the Holy Spirit, into living images of mercy.
May all come to know the depth of your mercy and sing the praises of your mercy forever. Amen.

CHAPTER 7

Objects of Faith

As human beings, we are both spiritual and physical, which means that it sometimes helps us to have sacred objects, such as medals, statues, icons, relics of the saints, votive candles, crucifixes, or holy water, which enable us to focus more intently on our prayer. These religious items are called sacramentals. Unlike the seven sacraments, a sacramental does not confer God's grace upon us, but the sacramental does make us open to receiving God's grace.

A sacramental should never replace our desire to celebrate the Eucharist and receive the other sacraments. A sacramental has no power in itself. The *Catechism of the Catholic Church* says the use of a sacramental must involve prayer, otherwise it slips into the realm of superstition.

The veneration of relics is a prime example of how a sacramental should and should not be used. Since the time of the early Christians, the bodies of saints and their belongings have been honored as reminders of a saint's holiness. The proper purpose of a relic, or any other sacramental, is to enhance our prayer life in ways that strengthen our faith in God — not as magical items that would force God or the saint to make something happen.

Pope Francis recognizes the importance of sacramentals in the prayer lives of Catholics. "I think of the steadfast faith of those mothers tending their sick children who, though perhaps barely familiar with the articles of the creed, cling to a rosary; or of all the hope poured into a candle lighted in a humble home with a prayer for help from Mary, or in the gaze of tender love directed to Christ crucified," Pope Francis says. "They are the manifestation of a theological life nourished by the working of the Holy Spirit who has been poured into our hearts."

The stories in this chapter illustrate some of the different ways people incorporate sacramentals into their prayer lives and the spiritual comfort that these sacramentals give to them.

Chasing Away Bad Dreams

When I was little and I had bad dreams, my mother would make the Sign of the Cross on my forehead with holy water and then sprinkle the holy water around the room. It chased away all of the bad dreams, and I felt safer knowing God was protecting me. Now I'm a mom, and I do the same thing with my two daughters. My prayer is that they will feel as loved and protected as I did, and I think they do!

— *Maggie Nolan*

HOLY WATER

Holy water reminds us of our baptismal promises, when we renounced Satan and were freed from original sin. We bless ourselves with holy water when we enter a church, and the priest blesses us with holy water during the Easter liturgies. Some people sprinkle their homes or their places of work with holy water as a way of asking God for a special blessing. There is also a long tradition in the Catholic Church that the use of holy water protects us against evil and temptations. In her *Autobiography*, Saint

Teresa of Ávila wrote, "From long experience I have learned that there is nothing like holy water to put devils to flight and prevent them from coming back again."

Praying with Icons

On a recent pilgrimage to the Holy Land, I decided to visit the Greek Orthodox church in Jerusalem. I had been there twenty-eight years before, and I remembered that they had fabulous icons painted all over the walls and ceiling. I had my camera, and I was trying to capture the essence of the building. When I got to the back of the church, I saw a priest seated in a chair. He stood up, tapped me on my shoulder, and said, "Excuse me. Are you a priest?"

I said yes.

He said, "You have come to my house and you haven't shown the honor of this being a holy place."

I said, "Excuse me?"

He said, "You didn't genuflect. You didn't bow your head. You didn't show reverence. You are caught behind your camera."

He took my hand, kissed it, and said, "A miracle happens in your hand every day when you celebrate the Divine Liturgy. You don't know what a gift you have."

Then he asked me twice that same question Jesus asked his disciples: "Do you know who I am?" As it turns out, this was no ordinary priest. He was the Patriarch of Jerusalem. So we talked, and he became for me that loving, compassionate God who says, "I love you unconditionally."

I went back the next day, and he was there. This time I tapped him on the shoulder and said, "I'm here today to pray."

I went up front, knelt down, and prayed in front of the iconostases for forty-five minutes. When I got up, he met me in the aisle and said, "I would like to take you on the other side of the icon screen." For the next twenty minutes, he explained the icons to me. Then he said, "Now you can bring out your camera and take your pictures. When you are done, turn off the lights and lock the door."

I expected to meet Jesus on this trip, but I met God himself in the Patriarch of Jerusalem. He saw inside my soul. He reminded me that I am a priest, and wherever I go I have to do the work that I am called to do, the work that I was meant to do. I came back a changed person.

— *Father Robert Wozniak*

WHAT IS AN ICON?

An icon is a mosaic or a painting that represents Jesus, Our Lady, a saint, or some sacred event. Icons are venerated as holy objects. They are sometimes called windows to the soul because the best way to pray with icons is to gaze upon them in silent contemplation. Icons are an important part of many churches, particularly in Eastern Europe, Russia, and the Middle East. An iconostasis is a wall decorated with icons that separates the sanctuary — where the Blessed Sacrament is reserved — from the main part of the church.

Burying Saint Joseph

My husband and I loved our little house in Charlotte, North Carolina. But after our first son was born, we both wanted to move back to Buffalo, New York, where we could be closer to our families. The problem was this was 2009, shortly after the housing crisis, and we had just purchased our home in 2007. We knew we had a very short window of time to sell our house, so we got really serious about it. I ordered a small Saint Joseph statue and buried him upside down next to our mailbox as I was instructed to do by the paperwork that came with him. Also in the instructions was a novena to Saint Joseph, and every morning with my coffee I prayed this novena.

Though it was stressful and frustrating to go through the process of selling our house with an infant, I trusted Saint Joseph and the process of prayer. Three months after we listed our house, it was sold!

Here's the crazy part. I really believe (and it has been my experience) that God sends us little confirmations to our answered prayers. As I looked over our closing paperwork, I saw our buyer's initials were STJ. My real estate agent, who was a close friend through this process, knew about my prayers to Saint Joseph, and when I pointed this out to her she gasped in surprise, "STJ … St. Joseph!" It was like God was telling us that he wanted this for us as much as we wanted it for ourselves.

According to the tradition of using Saint Joseph's help in selling or buying a home, you are supposed to display him in a place of honor in your new home. So I dug him up before we moved, and he now sits on a shelf in our dining room, overlooking our table. I like to thank him because our life has been so wonderful since we've been able to come home!

—*Jennifer Rychlicki*

WHY SAINT JOSEPH?

The tradition of burying a statue of Saint Joseph goes back to Saint Teresa of Ávila, who encouraged the Carmelite sisters to bury a medal of Saint Joseph and pray for his intercession when they needed to acquire more land for the convent. Saint André

Bessette buried a Saint Joseph medal on Mount Royal in Montreal, where the famous Saint Joseph's Oratory was later built. Today, plastic statues of Saint Joseph can be obtained through religious stores with instructions on how to bury the statue. Keep in mind, however, that unless burying a statue of Saint Joseph is accompanied by prayer, it is considered superstition. The point of this devotion is to pray to Saint Joseph for his help and intercession.

Do What Mother Teresa Would Do

In 2008, I was managing a small local radio station near Baton Rouge, Louisiana, with hopes of one day owning my own Catholic radio station. In late August that year, Hurricane Gustav hit south Louisiana and caused considerable damage. A few local radio stations were taken off the air as a result of the storm. One of them was a legendary AM station, WIBR, known for its history and signal strength.

I was very interested in purchasing WIBR. I was told it was for sale for $750,000, but that price did not include any equipment as everything was damaged beyond repair. The land where the towers were located was for lease at a rather high monthly expense. After doing the math, my three partners and I realized that it would take over $1 million just to get on the air — not including the high monthly overhead.

A small group of ladies from a local parish had been following our quest for a Catholic station and were praying for us. At a gathering where these women were in attendance, one of them pulled me aside and asked how our progress was going. I explained my dilemma with WIBR. The woman suggested that I simply do what Mother Teresa would do by placing a Miraculous Medal at the site and asking Our Lady for her intercession.

I obtained a Miraculous Medal for the purpose, but I was not exactly sure where the station's transmitter was located. One of my partners told me by phone how to get to the site. I followed his instructions and found myself looking at towers and a building that seemed to be in reasonable shape. I walked into the field, planted the Miraculous Medal, and prayed for Mary's guidance.

A short time later, I received an email from the Catholic Radio Association, telling me that an AM radio station was for sale in the Baton Rouge area. But the station they were talking about was not WIBR. It was a different station with the call letters WPYR. This new station was still functioning on the air. It was for sale — station, land, and equipment — all for $350,000.

I excitedly clicked on the coordinates of the towers and looked at the "street view" picture of the site. I knew it must be a mistake, as both the map and the picture for this new station showed the location of the towers where I had planted the medal.

I emailed the Catholic Radio Association and explained that the location they had listed as WPYR was really the location of WIBR. They responded with a map showing me the actual location of the WIBR towers a few miles up the road. I had prayed and planted the medal at the "wrong" towers!

On December 11, 2009, we closed on the purchase of WPYR, and thanks to Our Lady, Catholic Community Radio was born. Many, many other miracles have come our way since.

— *David Dawson*

SAINT TERESA OF CALCUTTA AND THE MIRACULOUS MEDAL

In 1830, Our Lady appeared to Saint Catherine Labouré and instructed her to have a medal cast with an image of the Immaculate Conception on the front and an image of the Crucifixion on the back. The medal became known as miraculous because of the number of physical healings and spiritual conversions associated with it. Saint Teresa of Calcutta was known for giving Miraculous Medals to everyone she encountered, urging them to pray, "Mother Mary, be a mother to me now."

Praying with Our Lady of Fátima

I had a replica of the Fátima statue of the Blessed Mother at my home for a week. On the first night, I called family and friends to visit. A priest came to lead the Rosary. My husband, Andrew, who had fallen away from the practice of his faith, said the Rosary with us, and it brought him back to the Catholic Church. Ever since that first day, Andrew and I have not missed saying the Rosary. The Blessed Mother has had a profound impact in our marriage and lives.

— *Maria Garrity*

TRAVELING STATUES OF OUR LADY

The tradition of a traveling statue, which began during medieval times, is rooted in the story of the birth of Jesus, when Mary and Joseph had to find shelter in a stable. In Bavaria, as part of a custom called *Frauentragen*, each family in the village hosts a statue or painting of Our Lady for one night in December. In Hispanic cultures, the custom is called *Posada*, and a statue of Our Lady is taken from home to home prior to Christmas. As the tradition grew, special traveling statues of Mary, such as Our Lady of Fátima, would be displayed in someone's home, where people would gather for prayers and devotions.

God Will Take Care of Me

When I was four years old, I was diagnosed with brain cancer. Through the prayers of my mother, my aunts, and my cousins, I came through brain surgery with no real side effects. I was very blessed to have a normal childhood.

When I was around thirty, a traveling priest came to our parish. After his talk, he invited us into the gym, where he had hundreds of relics from different saints on display. We were told that if we touched a medal or a holy card to one of the first-class relics, it would become a third-class relic.

I had the medal of Saint Elizabeth that I had received for my confirmation. I touched my medal to the relic of Saint Philomena, the patron saint of cancer patients. I thought that it would be good to have a third-class relic of this saint in case anyone I knew was diagnosed with cancer.

In the weeks that followed, I began to pray to Saint Philomena, an early Christian martyr whose tomb was discovered in the catacombs of Rome in 1802. I felt a strong desire to travel to the shrine where her body is entombed in Italy. Visiting the shrine was a very moving experience for me.

Six months later, I was diagnosed with brain cancer for the second time. I prayed to Saint Philomena, and I had a second miraculous surgery with no side effects. Then, unfortunately, a year later, I had a third recurrence and another brain surgery. Saint Philomena helped me through some very tough times. Through her, God has worked in my life to bring me deeper faith and peace. I have been healed, but not necessarily your typical physical healing that most people are looking for when they say, "She has been healed." God has done tremendous things with my soul and my faith.

Many times, people will tell me, "You have such strong faith. I know you're going to be fine." Not wanting to burst their bubble, I just say, "Thank you." The truth is, I have faith that God will take care of me. That doesn't mean cancer might not end my journey here on earth. But no matter what happens, I know that in this life or in the next, I will be fine.

— *Emily Weimer*

Emily Weimer lost her battle with cancer and entered into eternal life on October 11, 2016.

THE THREE TYPES OF RELICS

A first-class relic is from the body of a saint, such as a piece of bone or hair. A second-class relic is an object that was used by a saint, perhaps a piece of clothing or a prayer book. A third-class relic is an object that was reverently touched to a first- or second-class relic. Relics are always considered sacred objects, because they remind us of the powerful way in which God worked through the lives of the saints.

CHAPTER 8

Praying with Our Lady

Devotions to the Blessed Mother have always been popular among Catholics. But Marian devotions are often misunderstood by some Protestants, who assume that Catholics worship Mary as a kind of goddess. Nothing could be further from the truth!

Catholics believe that Mary holds a place of esteem because she was selected by God to be the mother of Jesus. But because Mary was also fully human, Catholics see her as a role model, a real person, who experienced many of the same questions, challenges, emotions, and painful moments that we all face in life. In their prayers and devotions, Catholics ask Mary to pray for them and to present their intentions to her Son. Mary is the beacon that points the way to Jesus.

Pope Francis encourages Catholics to pray to Our Lady. "In our life, we are not alone; we have the constant help and companionship of the Virgin Mary," he explains. "Today she stands before us as first among the saints, the first disciple of the Lord. We flee to her protection and to her we present our sorrows and our joys, our fears and our aspirations. We put everything under her protection, in the sure knowledge that she watches over us and cares for us with a mother's love."

The Rosary is probably the most common Catholic devotion to Our Lady. But there are also special prayers, consecrations, and novenas that are popular among Catholics. The stories in this chapter reveal some of the ways Catholics ask Our Lady to bring them into a closer relationship with Jesus.

THE PRAYER OF MARY

The following prayer from the Gospel of Luke was Mary's joy-filled response when she visited her cousin Elizabeth. It is commonly known as the Magnificat:

My soul magnifies the Lord,
and my spirit rejoices in God my Savior,
for he has regarded the low estate of his handmaiden.
For behold, henceforth all generations will call me
blessed;
for he who is mighty has done great things for me,
and holy is his name.
And his mercy is on those who fear him
from generation to generation.
He has shown strength with his arm,
he has scattered the proud in the imagination of their
hearts,
he has put down the mighty from their thrones,
and exalted those of low degree;
he has filled the hungry with good things,
and the rich he has sent empty away.
He has helped his servant Israel,
in remembrance of his mercy,
as he spoke to our fathers,
to Abraham and to his posterity for ever. (Luke 1:46–55)

One Thousand Hail Marys

When I was fourteen, I was very concerned because my father did not go to church. My mother was Protestant. My brother and I both went to Catholic school.

Someone told me that if you said one thousand Hail Marys on Good Friday, you would get whatever you wanted. So I said the Hail Marys on Good Friday, and I prayed that my father would start going back to church.

The following Monday my brother, who is five years younger than I am, ruptured his appendix. He was rushed to the hospital and immediately taken into surgery. My father promised God that he would go back to church if my brother recovered. Fortunately, the puss did not spread through my brother's body. It formed a ball on his appendix. For some reason, the surgeon could not remove both, so he removed the ball of puss, and they had to go back later to remove his appendix.

You can imagine the guilt I felt as a fourteen-year-old, thinking that my prayer had caused my little brother all of this pain! My brother eventually recovered. My father kept his promise, and every Sunday he went to Mass with us. Years later, my brother and I reminisce with fondness about how we both did our part to get our father back to church!

— *Sister Marianne Ferguson, O.S.F.*

THE HAIL MARY

The Hail Mary is a Scripture-based prayer. The first sentence of the prayer is based on the angel Gabriel's words to Mary in Luke's Gospel (Luke 1:28). The second sentence is based on Elizabeth's greeting to Mary (Luke 1:42). The final sentence, a prayer asking Our Lady to pray for us now and at the hour of our death, was added in the sixteenth century.

The Power of the Rosary

Several years ago, my doctor ordered a stress test. Considering the fact that all four of my brothers had heart or vascular issues, I was nervous. After the stress test, I was told that they wanted to check further. They scheduled me for another test.

I try to say the Rosary on a consistent basis, but I am not always diligent. Well, when I got the news about another test, I picked up my pace, and I prayed the Rosary every day with more fervor. One day while praying, I felt a warmth in the left side of my breastbone. Shortly thereafter, I had the test and everything was fine. The doctor later said he was a bit surprised because he expected to find a blockage on my left side.

Was it the power of prayer? The power of the Rosary? I think so!

— *Mike Reilly*

THE ROSARY

According to legend, Our Lady gave the Rosary to Saint Dominic in the thirteenth century, but the practice of using beads to pray Our Fathers actually started in monasteries during the Middle Ages. Eventually, five decades of Hail Marys and the Joyful, Sorrowful, and Glorious Mysteries from the life of Jesus were added, making the Rosary not just a recitation of prayers but also a meditation on the life of Christ. Saint John Paul II added the five Luminous Mysteries that reflect key events in the public ministry of Jesus.

Our Prayers Kept Us Going

When my children were young, we planned a two-hour road trip to an amusement park in Canada. When we started off that morning, my husband noticed the car was not acting right. He thought we should turn around and go back home, but our children were so disappointed that I suggested that we give it a try.

At first everything seemed okay. We crossed the Peace Bridge from the United States into Canada and were heading toward Toronto when the car started acting up again. We had to stop every fifteen minutes. We realized at this point that we had made a terrible mistake, but it was too late to turn back.

We finally arrived at the amusement park and spent the day trying not to think about our trip home. The car seemed fine when we were ready to leave, which gave us hope. As we started to go over the Peace Bridge back into the United States, cars were backed up at the customs booths, which meant our car would be idling in stop-and-go traffic — not good! If our car broke down on the bridge, it would be a disaster, not just for us, but for all of the cars around us!

I asked the children and my husband to pray the Rosary with me. The car started to sound a little better, so we kept praying the Rosary all the way home. We never had to stop once! The car made it back home and then died in our driveway. I know our faith and prayers kept us going. The children are all grown up now, but they never forgot the power of their prayers that day.

— *Marguerite Sammarco*

Do You Mind if We Pray a Rosary Together?

My fiancé and I had recently broken our engagement. I was in the college chapel and I prayed, "I've had it, God! I stay away from wild parties. I spend weekends working on college retreats. But what good does it do? You've got to tell me who to marry. I will pray a Rosary every day until you do."

A trickle of peace began to fill my emptiness. Still, I was a little surprised at myself. A Rosary?

As I walked out of the chapel, I met John. He was part of the college retreat team. He told me that he and his fiancée had just broken their engagement. As the weeks and months passed by, I prayed the Rosary, asking God who to marry. I had never gotten this concrete with God before. How would he tell me? Would I hear a voice? How would I recognize the right guy?

I kept expecting an answer, but nothing came. Sometimes distractions crept in. Like the time I found myself stewing about working on a retreat with John, the tall guy from the chapel that day.

"I don't even like John," I complained. "I wish I could work with somebody else."

Like him or not, we worked together a lot that winter and spring. He would give me rides home in his dad's station wagon. One night he said, "I know it's late, but would you mind if we prayed a Rosary together?"

"Strange," I thought. Then my heart skipped a beat. "Oh no," I silently prayed. "You've got to be kidding, God. It's probably a coincidence. After all, I don't even like him."

John and I prayed the Rosary together that night, and several more times as spring turned to summer. Along the way we became friends, and then more than friends. Love dissolved my petty dislikes.

One night in August, John asked me to marry him. A joyful peace surrounded us in his dad's car. Then John asked, "Do you mind if we pray a Rosary together?"

"Of course not!" I replied. "But why do you like to pray the Rosary so much?"

"When I broke up with my fiancée," John explained, "I decided to pray the Rosary until God showed me who to marry. Tonight, I'd just like to thank God for answering."

— *Therese Boucher*

What Is God's Will for Me?

I had broken up with my boyfriend that spring, and I didn't want to date anyone. I had started to think that God was calling me to the single life. Our parish priest suggested that I could open a house of discernment for single people. But before I made a commitment to anything new, I had to find out what God's will was for me, because clearly, my way wasn't working.

My mother's friend gave me a little prayer book called *Rosary Novenas to Our Lady*. She had prayed this novena and said it was very powerful.

My friend Dan and I decided to pray the novena together. He was also at a crossroads in his life. He was trying to discern whether he had a vocation to priesthood or married life.

We both started the novena, which is not a normal novena of nine days, but instead involves twenty-seven days of petition followed by twenty-seven days of thanksgiving. Each day you pray the Rosary, along with some additional prayers. The booklet said you had to complete the entire novena, even if your prayers have not been answered.

Halfway through the thanksgiving part of the novena, I realized that God was asking me to totally surrender, so I let go of all control and promised not to hold anything back. I took it as a sign that I was now ready for whatever God was going to give to me.

I met Tom in August. His brother introduced us after Mass. I barely made eye contact with him because I was still thinking that God was calling me to the single life. For the next four or five weeks, Tom made it a point to talk to me after Mass.

Finally, one day as we were walking out of church, he asked if I would like to have dinner. I really was not interested, but I agreed. After that date, I found myself hoping that he would call again. He did call. We went out on two more dates.

After our third date, I had the most calm and peaceful vision of seeing sand and water forever. I knew that it was a sign that we were meant to be together. Tom was the answer to my prayers. We were married the following year, and our lives have been blessed.

— *Carrie Duquin*

ROSARY NOVENAS TO OUR LADY

This little prayer book was published in 1924, and it calls for a serious commitment to praying the Rosary along with additional prayers in the booklet every day for fifty-four days. The book is called *Rosary Novenas* because the petitioner actually makes six novenas of nine days each. During the first three novenas, you state your petition; during the next three novenas, you offer thanksgiving to God — whether or not your prayer has been answered. The booklet warns that all prayers are answered, but not always in the way we expect.

Trust Him

I started singing at Mass when I was in elementary school. By the time I was in high school, people were asking me to sing for weddings and funerals. I always got nervous when I had to do a solo — not just a little nervous, but sick-to-my-stomach nervous. I would often pray, "Lord, you have given me this gift, and so many people have complimented me, but I get so nervous. Help me get over this!"

The answer to my prayer came when the women's group in my parish decided to consecrate ourselves to Our Lady using the book *33 Days to Morning Glory* by Father Michael Gaitley,

M.I.C. The consecration changed my life. I felt as if Our Lady took my hand, put it on the heart of Jesus, and said, "Trust him." I suddenly realized that I had been holding myself in bondage and tying myself down to high expectations of myself. I was worried about what other people would think.

As I was making this consecration, I felt as if Mary said, "So what if you make a mistake! It's no big deal. God knows where your heart is. He knows that what you do is all for his glory. You are worshipping him. Everyone is equal. You are not better than anyone. No one is better than you."

Instantly, I felt a wave of peace and freedom.

Before this, I was not writing songs. After my first session of Marian consecration, I sat at the piano and I prayed to the Blessed Mother. Then I wrote a song based on the Marian consecration. I was so overwhelmed that I started crying. I did not know where this music was coming from. Now I know that it was Mary. I was her instrument. Mary was just waiting for me to be ready and open. I've written so many prayer songs since then. All of this music is just pouring out of me.

It is so powerful when you surrender. It is a letting go and really trusting. It's not like I trust 100 percent all of the time. I struggle every day like everybody else, but when I do trust, the graces just pour into my life.

— *Anna Nuzzo*

CONSECRATION TO JESUS THROUGH MARY

Throughout the centuries, various forms of consecration to Jesus through Mary have been used as a way of growing into deeper union with Christ. A number of religious communities consecrate themselves to Our Lady. The Carmelites wear the brown scapular as a sign of their consecration. Saint Louis de Montfort introduced a total consecration to Our Lady in the eighteenth century.

Saint John Paul II popularized consecration to the Immaculate Heart of Mary. "Our act of consecration refers ultimately to the heart of her Son," he explained, "for as the Mother of Christ she is wholly united to his redemptive mission. As at the marriage feast of Cana, when she said, 'Do whatever he tells you,' Mary directs all things to her Son, who answers our prayers and forgives our sins. Thus by dedicating ourselves to the heart of Mary we discover a sure way to the Sacred Heart of Jesus, symbol of the merciful love of our Savior."

Mary, Will You Walk with Me Today?

A lot of people in our parish were consecrating themselves to Mary, but I felt that it was not quite my time. I was still growing in my faith. I wasn't ready.

After a while, I finally decided to do it. I consecrated myself to Our Lady on New Year's Day, the feast of Mary, the Mother of God. I can't even describe the peace that came with it.

What always brings me back is that Mary was human. I can relate to her as a human person. We still have a little disconnect with Jesus because he is God. But I can totally relate to Mary. Everything we experience she experienced two thousand years ago — in a different way and time — but history repeats itself. I just ask her, "Mary, will you walk with me today? You know what I am going through. Help lead me to your Son, Jesus."

She is always there for me. A lot of guys think it is effeminate to consecrate themselves to Mary, but we all have a mother, and we all need Mary to be our mother as well.

— *Mike Nuzzo*

DO YOU WANT TO BE WELL?

In 2008, I was diagnosed with bladder cancer. The diagnosis was verified by three different hospitals, and the doctors agreed that I required major surgery. My wife and I decided that we would do nothing until we asked our Blessed Mother what to do.

After some very generous help from parishioners, my wife and I visited Lourdes in southwestern France, where Our Lady appeared to Saint Bernadette in 1858. I prayed, participated in the Rosary procession, and washed in the baths. I served as a deacon at Masses in the grotto, in the underground church, and in the side chapel. I didn't pray for a cure, only for direction, for Our Lady's intercession, and for my protection.

At that time, there were outdoor "water" stations along the opposite side of the river from the grotto, which described various Scripture stories that involved water. I prayed at each station. The last station was the story of Jesus and the blind man at the pool of Bethesda (John 5). The blind man had no one to help him into the healing waters. Jesus asked: "Do you want to be well?" I heard those words spoken directly to me at that very moment.

Suddenly I knew what direction we should take, and I knew that the Blessed Mother would be with me every step of the way. We flew home, and I had the surgery in late October, followed by chemotherapy. I have been in remission since 2009 — all glory and honor to our merciful Father and his mother.

Now the rest of the story: We went on a pilgrimage to Rome for the Jubilee of Deacons with Pope Francis, and we took a side trip to Lourdes. I can't describe my excitement and anticipation to revisit the place where my miracle of words and encouragement occurred. I began to weep at my very first step on the site. I was almost running to the grotto to fall on my knees in thanksgiving for the gift I received through Mary's intercession. I was disappointed that the "water stations" had been destroyed by a flood. But I prayed, served at Mass in the grotto, and went to the baths again. I was almost delirious with joy and thanksgiving. I know that our Blessed Virgin Mary interceded on my behalf.

I share this story, not because it is an exceptional story of healing, but it is for me a story of hope and a story of a prayer being answered.

— *Deacon John DeWolfe*

GOING ON A PILGRIMAGE

From early Christianity to the present day, Catholics have traveled to sacred places to pray. One of the most popular places of pilgrimage is Lourdes, in southwestern France, where Our Lady appeared to Saint Bernadette Soubirous in 1858. Since that time, the Catholic Church has affirmed that many miracle cures have occurred after people bathed in the springs.

A Calmness Entered His Body

My brother, Joe, was diagnosed with Crohn's disease when he was a young adult. Joe dealt with a great deal of pain and suffering for many years. Then, Joe and my sister, Jeanette, took a pilgrimage to Lourdes, France. As they were praying, my brother was submerged into the holy spring water. Joe said a calmness entered his body. His symptoms seemed to diminish each day after visiting Lourdes. Joe is now in remission with minor if any symptoms of the disease. He is only taking preventative medicine. We owe this all to the power of prayer, and we are thankful each day for our Catholic faith.

— *Maria Garrity*

PRAYER TO OUR LADY OF LOURDES

O ever Immaculate Virgin, Mother of mercy, health of the sick, refuge of sinners, comfort of the afflicted, you know my wants, my troubles, my sufferings; deign to cast upon me a look of mercy. By appearing in the Grotto of Lourdes, you were pleased to make it a privileged sanctuary, whence you dispense your favors, and already many sufferers have obtained the cure of their infirmities both spiritual and corporal. I come, therefore, with unbounded confidence, to implore your maternal intercession. Obtain, O loving Mother, the grant of my requests. I will endeavor to imitate your virtues, that I may one day share your glory, and bless you in eternity. Amen.

I Have to Be a Marian Priest

I decided to become a Catholic in 1992 after a pretty radical conversion. At that point, I didn't know what I was going to do with the rest of my life. So I started to go to church every morning where I would pray the Rosary before Mass. I prayed with the intention, "Lord, I owe you everything. I'll do whatever you want. But I don't know what I am supposed to do. You've given me my life back, and now I give my life to you. What do you want me to do?"

I assumed that I would meet a girl and get married, but the more I prayed the Rosary, the more I felt attracted to the priesthood. I'd be meditating on the mysteries of the Rosary, and then we would have Mass, and I began to feel drawn to what the priest was doing on the altar. Once I sensed that I was being called to the priesthood, I began to pray, "Well, Lord, if you want me to be a priest, I have to be a Marian priest. I have to be devoted to Our Lady. But there are so many Marian communities out there, I don't know what you want me to do."

I sent out a whole stack of postcards to vocation directors in various religious communities. The first response that I received back was from the "Marians of the Immaculate Conception of the Most Blessed Virgin Mary." I was amazed. This community had Our Lady's name three times in their title! I decided they must be really serious about their love for Mary, so I went and checked them out. The rest is history. I never went to any other place.

It was definitely through the daily Rosary that God answered my prayers for what my vocation would be. Ever since then, the Rosary is in my pocket. I don't go anywhere without it. The Rosary is my companion. It has been so helpful in asking for direction and receiving guidance.

— *Father Donald Calloway, M.I.C.*

CHAPTER 9

Saints Alive!

Many Catholics think of saints as their special friends in heaven. It is not unusual to hear some Catholics speak as if they have a special relationship with a saint — especially if that person has the same name as the saint.

That Catholics pray to saints is a source of contention with some Protestants, who rightly claim that only God can answer prayers. What they don't understand, however, is that, technically, Catholics don't pray to a saint to grant them a favor or to help in some way. Instead, Catholics ask the saint to pray to God on their behalf, just as someone would ask a friend or a family member to pray to God for them.

The practice of spiritual connection with saints began in the very early days of the Church. On the walls of the catacombs, early Christians wrote inscriptions asking Saint Peter and Saint Paul to pray for them. During medieval times, devotions to the saints flourished, and for many Catholics special devotions to the saints continue to this day.

Pope Francis tells us that "saints are men and women who enter fully into the mystery of prayer. Men and women who struggle with prayer, letting the Holy Spirit pray and struggle in them. They struggle to the very end, with all their strength, and they triumph, but not by their own efforts: the Lord triumphs in them and with them.... Through their example and their intercession, may God also enable us to be men and women of prayer."

Here are several stories of ordinary Catholics, who sought the help of saints in a variety of different circumstances.

PATRON SAINTS

A patron saint is chosen as a spiritual advocate for a country, a city, an occupation, or an individual. Saints are often named patrons of places where they were born or where they lived and ministered. Saint Patrick, for example, is the patron saint of Ireland. Many trades or professions also have patron saints. For instance, Saint Lawrence is the patron saint of chefs. Saint Elizabeth Ann Seton is the patron saint of Catholic schools. Saint Francis de Sales is the patron saint of journalists. It is common for parish churches to be named after saints, making their namesake their special patron. Many Catholics claim as their patron a saint who shares their name. Some Catholics choose a saint's name when they receive the Sacrament of Confirmation, and that saint also becomes a patron for them.

She Sent Me a Rose

On October 1, the feast day of Saint Thérèse of Lisieux, my third-grade teacher read us some stories of people who had prayed to her and were sent a rose when their prayer was answered. Our teacher gave us a moment to say our own prayers to Saint Thérèse afterwards.

I was maybe eight years old, and my mom was sick with a virus. I didn't really understand. All I knew was that it made her extremely tired, and she spent most of her evenings and weekends in bed, unable to play with me and my sister. I later learned it was the Epstein-Barr virus. So while I wasn't sure what to pray for at first, my mom came to mind, and I sent my prayer to Saint Thérèse. I asked her to heal my mom — to make her healthy and energetic again, and to allow her to be well enough to enjoy an upcoming vacation our family had planned.

That afternoon, I was at my grandmother's house doing my homework at her kitchen table. When I looked out her back window, I saw something pink. I asked my grandmother if she knew what it was, and she said she didn't know, but we could go outside and look. When we got out there, we saw a single, perfect, pink rose on an old, overgrown rose bush. This was October, so it definitely shouldn't have been there! The funny thing is, my grandmother was even shorter than I was at the time, and the rose was up high, so neither of us could reach it.

I told her the story of my prayers to Saint Thérèse of Lisieux at school that day. I grew up in a very Polish-Catholic family, so my grandmother immediately understood, and she believed that Saint Thérèse of Lisieux had heard my prayer. I remember my grandmother telling me that it was okay that we couldn't reach the pink rose. God would know we saw it, and we should just stand and admire its beauty for a few minutes.

When my mom picked me up that day, she was in a great mood. I don't know if my grandmother told her our story or not, but for a few days I smugly held onto my little secret to watch and see if my mom was improving. When she finally mentioned how good she was feeling, I said, "That was me! I did that!" I proudly told her my story. She had improved so quickly, and her energy was so much better after that!

My mother and I both love to tell that story because I barely knew what I was asking for that day or how desperately my mother needed help. I was just a little kid who wanted my mom to play with me. So I thought of my mom when my teacher told me some lady in heaven would send me a rose if I asked her for what was in my heart!

—Jennifer Rychlicki

SAINT THÉRÈSE OF LISIEUX

Saint Thérèse of Lisieux (1873–1897) was a Carmelite nun, whose autobiography, *The Story of a Soul*, touched the minds and hearts of Catholics all over the world because of the simplicity of her spirituality. In 1997 Pope Saint John Paul II named her a doctor of the Church. She is also known as the "Little Flower of Jesus" because she saw herself as a tiny flower in God's garden. Before she died from tuberculosis at age twenty-four, she promised to spend her time in heaven doing good things on earth. On her deathbed she said, "I will let fall a shower of roses."

For the Glory of God

In the early 1980s, my husband and I desperately wanted a child, but my medical condition made conception unlikely. I turned to Saint Francis Xavier and the Novena of Grace in his honor, which involves nine days of prayer from March 4 through March 12.

This novena originated in the seventeenth century. A Jesuit priest who struggled with a serious head injury sought the intercession of Saint Francis Xavier. The priest heard an interior voice promising that anyone who prayed a nine-day novena to Saint Francis Xavier would receive the saint's protection, and the assurance that any request would be granted provided it was for that person's good and for the glory of God. After praying a novena to Saint Francis Xavier, the priest recovered.

When I prayed the novena, I asked that the Lord would grant my husband and me the gift of a child. Four months later, I conceived our son. He was born the following March, and we named him Joseph Patrick Xavier.

Over the years I would often pray the novena during the month of March. Last year, I prayed the novena for my niece, who had undergone cancer treatments; for my nephew, who was applying for certification as a teacher; and for my son, who was undergoing medical tests. The novena asks that you attend Mass and receive Communion at least once during the nine days of prayer. But I was so focused on my prayer requests that I made it a point to go to Mass every day.

At the end of the novena, all of my intentions were granted. My niece was free of cancer. My nephew received his certification. And my son received a clean bill of health. Thank you, Saint Francis Xavier!

— *Marianne Hanley*

SAINT FRANCIS XAVIER

Saint Francis Xavier (1506–1552) was a companion of Saint Ignatius of Loyola and was one of the first members of the Society of Jesus. As a missionary, he traveled to Asia, working primarily in India, but also in Japan, Borneo, and the Maluku Islands. He died on Shangchuan Island in 1552. He was canonized on March 12, 1622.

How Saint Anthony Found Bob's Glasses

It was a gorgeous day for a boat ride on the lake. All seven grandchildren, three daughters, two sons-in-law, and one dog boarded the family pontoon boat. Suddenly, the boat slowed down to a halt, the anchor was dropped, and my son-in-law, Bob, shouted, "Let's go swimming!" Eight heads disappeared overboard.

All of a sudden Bob's head popped up from the water with a cry. "I lost my glasses!" He was so accustomed to wearing them that he forgot to take them off when he jumped in the water! Everyone was silent, but all of us had the same question on our minds. How would we ever be able to find Bob's glasses?

Finally, I said, "We will find them because we will pray to St. Anthony, the saint who always finds lost articles." To myself I prayed, "St. Anthony, you have a real job on your hands!"

A decision was made. Two of us would stay on the inflatable raft to mark the spot. The rest would head back to pick up goggles and a flash light. I decided to stay home and say some additional prayers. Before I could finish my Rosary, I heard voices. I ran to the dock and called out, "Did you find the glasses?"

A chorus of voices called, "Yes!"

"Did you remember to thank St. Anthony?"

Again, a chorus of voices called back, "Yes, we did!"

— *Nancy Allaire Donohue*

A SAINT IN CHARGE OF LOST OBJECTS?

Saint Anthony of Padua (1195–1231) is called the patron saint of lost objects. This tradition stems from an incident involving a novice who took Saint Anthony's favorite prayer book. Saint

Anthony prayed that the book would be found, and the guilty novice returned the book.

Singing to St. Anthony

When my children were growing up, and one of us lost something, we would sing, "Dear St. Anthony, please come around. Something's lost and can't be found."

Years later, I lost my diamond earrings. I was very upset until my five-year-old granddaughter, Abby, left a voicemail on my phone: "Don't worry, Nonna. We sang to St. Anthony. He'll find your earrings for you."

Needless to say, I found the earrings! And I saved that voicemail until I had to get a new phone.

— *Terri Ferrari*

A Novena to Saint Gerard

For the first part of our marriage, my husband, Cory, and I struggled to have children. We were married for seven years before I became pregnant with our first child. Aidan Richard Busse was born happy and healthy on October 22, 2004. I remember holding Aidan and memorizing every hair on his head. Cory and I knew we were called to have more children.

I found out I was pregnant again about a year and a half after Aidan was born. Sadly, that pregnancy ended in a miscarriage. We tried again and experienced another miscarriage, this time later into the pregnancy than before.

The grief and stigma of miscarriage is overwhelming. In the midst of our grief, I started a novena to Saint Gerard. I prayed for a brother or sister for Aidan, and I specifically prayed for God to give us the soul that we were meant to raise. When we found out we were pregnant again a year later, Cory and I were cautiously optimistic. We didn't tell our family or friends right away, for fear that we might lose another baby. Once we found out we were having a girl, we decided to name her Amelia. We didn't tell anyone her name.

As we were drawing close to her birth, I received a call from my aunt who said she had had a dream that we would be having a girl, and that the baby would bring us great joy — and that her name would be Amelia! It was a like a prophecy from the Old Testament. I knew this was the soul we were meant to have.

Amelia Joy Busse was born on October 2, 2007. She is a feisty redhead with deep faith. Aidan is a bright, kind, cerebral young man. Our kids are our light and life, and I know they are an answer to our prayers.

— *Heidi Busse*

SAINT GERARD MAJELLA

Saint Gerard Majella (1726–1755) was born in Muro, Italy, to a poor family. At age twenty-three, he joined the Congregation of the Most Holy Redeemer and eventually became known as a miracle worker. After his death, a young woman unexpectedly went into labor and was on the verge of losing her baby when she asked for Saint Gerard's handkerchief to be laid on her stomach. The pain stopped, and she gave birth to a healthy baby. Saint Gerard's prayers are now sought by expectant mothers and couples who long for a child.

Prayer to Saint Gerard for the Birth of a Child

O good Saint Gerard, powerful intercessor before the throne of God, wonder-worker of our day, I call upon you and seek your help. While on earth, you always fulfilled God's designs; help me, too, always do God's holy will. Beseech the master of life, from whom all parenthood proceeds, to bless me with offspring, that I may raise up children to God in this life and heirs to the kingdom of God's glory in the life to come. Amen.

Saint Joseph Came Through

One February evening, my husband came home from work and told me that headquarters was moving people to branch offices. "What do you think about Cleveland?" he asked.

I was happy living in Virginia. Life was good. But I had such a sense of peace deep in my soul that I knew moving to Cleveland was God's will. My husband was not nearly as confident that we were supposed to go. He began a novena asking for a definitive sign. He finished the novena on Wednesday. The next day he went into a meeting where his boss unexpectedly announced that he was removing my husband from his position, giving it to someone else, and assigning my husband to a position which he had previously held and absolutely hated. My husband had his sign.

On the Monday of Holy Week, my husband accepted an offer to move to Cleveland. A colleague recommended a suburb called Lakewood. I dove into research. By Holy Thursday morning, I had exhausted my efforts to learn about Lakewood. At 9:00 that morning, I told Jesus, "It looks perfect. It's a short commute for my husband, 100 percent sidewalks, two Catholic schools, plus a lot of beautiful, historic homes. But Jesus, I don't know about the parishes. Are they good?"

Our primary concern was being able to raise children in the Catholic faith, and we needed a solid parish to do that. There were four in Lakewood. About 10:45 that same morning, my dad called. He had just gotten off the phone with a priest friend who had only one parish recommendation: St. Clement Church.

Now we just needed to sell our house in Virginia and find a new one in Ohio. We prayed a novena to Saint Joseph (although we did not bury him upside down). We asked Saint Joseph to sell our house by July 3, and I had an exact amount in my head that I wanted it to sell for. Our real estate agent thought the amount and date were a little ambitious, but he said he would try.

We listed our house on June 26. On the morning of July 3, we got a full-price offer. Saint Joseph came through.

Now on to the Ohio house. Again, we prayed to Saint Joseph, and again, I was specific: we needed a house by July 19, and I wanted a Divine Mercy image to be associated with the house as confirmation that it was the right one!

We arrived in Ohio for the house-hunting trip, and things were rather disappointing. By July 18, we had seen all the houses listed, and there was nothing. But, it wasn't July 19 yet. Saint Joseph had one more day.

I asked my husband if he would mind if I went to pray and regain some perspective. I thought one of the local parishes had Mass at 5:00 p.m. I was wrong, but the church was open, so I decided to pray before the tabernacle. As I knelt down, I looked to the right of the tabernacle and there was a picture of the Divine Mercy. I looked up and there was a statue of Saint Joseph.

When I returned to our hotel room, my husband showed me a website with a house that had come on the market a little after 5 p.m., while I was praying in the church. It was our dream house, and it was within a block of St. Clement Catholic Church! God was faithful.

Now our prayer is that we will be faithful to his plans for us.

— *Gianna Davis*

SAINT JOSEPH

Saint Joseph is the patron saint of families, fathers, house-hunters, travelers, cabinetmakers, carpenters, workers, Canada, dying people, and the Universal Church.

I Prayed for Three Things

I was ending my assignment as parochial vicar at the cathedral and I did not know where I would be sent next. I had planned a trip to Washington, D.C., because I wanted to visit the Saint John Paul II National Shrine. While I was there, I knelt in front of the relic of Saint John Paul II and I prayed for three things:

First, I asked that in my next assignment, I would go where I could best use my gifts as a priest.

Second, because of a previous medical exam, a follow-up procedure was scheduled, and I prayed for good results.

Third, I asked to find peace.

When I returned from the trip, I had the medical procedure done, and a short time later, the rector of the seminary asked if I would consider accepting the position of Director of Formation for the seminarians. He said he saw in me a love for the priesthood and how I lived it out in my daily life. He wanted that role model for our seminarians.

This offer came out of the blue. I had always loved parish ministry and had never even thought about the seminary. But there was no way I could make a decision until I received the results of my medical procedure.

The following Sunday a nurse from my doctor's office called in tears. I immediately expected bad news, but these were tears of joy! "They found nothing!" she told me.

All of this was overwhelming. I told the rector of the seminary that I wanted to consult with the bishop before making a final decision on becoming the Director of Formation. The bishop's secretary scheduled me for an appointment on the feast of Saint John Paul II.

I told the bishop about my visit to Washington, my three prayers, and my appointment with him on Saint John Paul II's feast day. He encouraged me to accept the position at the seminary. I felt a deep sense of peace. I have been back to the Pope John Paul II shrine three times in gratitude. My three prayers were answered.

— *Father Robert Wozniak*

THE SAINT JOHN PAUL II NATIONAL SHRINE

The Saint John Paul II National Shrine in Washington, D.C., is a place of pilgrimage where people can attend Mass, receive the sacraments, seek pastoral care, participate in educational and cultural activities, and learn about the life and teachings of Saint John Paul II, who was canonized on April 27, 2014, by Pope Francis.

CHAPTER 10

Lead Me, Lord

Praying for guidance and asking for strength are just a few of the many ways we seek God's help. These are always dangerous prayers, however, because in the process of praying, we surrender our own will and humbly ask God to lead us in whatever direction he chooses.

Sometimes, God affirms what we hoped would happen. It is almost as if God knows the deepest desires of our hearts, and what we want is also God's will for us. But there are also times when we really don't know what to do, and we trust that God will give us some indication of what his will is for us.

Surrender to God's will is the essence of authentic spirituality. It involves emptying yourself of everything that is not important, and in the process of emptying yourself, you allow God to fill the empty spaces with his loving presence.

"Do I pray that the Lord gives me the desire to do his will, or do I look for compromises because I'm afraid of God's will?" Pope Francis asks. "Another thing: praying to know God's will for me and my life, concerning a decision that I must take now.... And when I know God's will, praying again for the third time, to follow it. To carry out that will, which is not my own, it is his will. And all this is not easy."

One of the best ways to begin this kind of relationship with God is to meditate on the powerful words from Proverbs:

Trust in the LORD with all your heart
    and do not rely on your own insight,
In all your ways acknowledge him,
    and he will make straight your paths.
(Proverbs 3:5–6)

The stories in this chapter illustrate some of the vastly different ways that people asked the Lord to lead them, and the astounding ways in which God answered their prayers.

Why Am I Here?

After I retired, my friend invited me to go on a weekend retreat for people who might be interested in ministry at a women's prison. When I got there, I was asked, "Why did you come?"

I replied, "I really don't know."

After that, I started praying, "Lord, why am I here? What do you want me to do?"

The next day there was a bundle of notes from team members inviting us to join this ministry. I got a note from a woman that was written entirely in calligraphy. I had just started taking calligraphy lessons, so I was intrigued. As I read the letter, I began to sob. She talked about the brokenness, the pain, and the suffering experienced by women in prison. She talked about how many women are set up by men and left holding the bag. It was like God touching my heart about the suffering and telling me that I was being called to this ministry.

I worked my first Kairos weekend in November 2003. I was assigned outside a women's prison to pray for the team members who were ministering to the inmates. The following year, I became part of the team that goes inside the prison. I have grown to love the ladies in the prison, and they know I love them. I also facilitate a Catholic Bible study for them in addition to the Kairos weekends. Throughout all of this, I keep talking to the Lord.

— *Carolyn McLean*

WHAT IS KAIROS PRISON MINISTRY?

Kairos Prison Ministry began in 1976 and offers four days of prayer and reflection for people in prisons. The Greek word "*Kairos*" means "in God's special time." A prison-ministry weekend begins on a Thursday night and continues until Sunday. Prior to that, there are five Saturdays of team-building so the ministry team can go into the prison with a loving sense of friendship and camaraderie. The Kairos ministry was developed in response to the words of Jesus, "I was in prison and you came to me" (Matthew 25:36).

An Impossible Prayer

In 1977, I received word that Father James Keller had died, and the Catholic multimedia organization he founded, The Christophers, was searching for a new director. My heart leapt! I had admired Father James Keller ever since my father gave me his book, *You Can Change the World,* on my eighteenth birthday.

Right then and there, I prayed an impossible prayer: "Dear Lord, help me to become Father Keller's successor."

The reason this desire welled up in my heart was clear to me. When I was going to Fordham University in New York, I became an announcer on their radio station, hoping to prepare myself for a career in the media. All that changed when I decided to become a priest. Eighteen years after my ordination, I was serving as a pastor and as the chief judge of the Marriage Tribunal in the Diocese of Paterson, New Jersey. That's when I heard of Father Keller's death. Even though I prayed to succeed him, I took no action. I was too busy, and besides I had no experience running a media organization.

Three weeks later I suddenly thought, "What have I got to lose?"

So I wrote a letter to The Christophers' Board of Directors, applying for the position. It took one year from the time I applied for the job until the board actually chose me to be their new director. I was jubilant.

I served as director of The Christophers for nearly eighteen years. Bringing the Christopher message to millions was a profound joy, and I thank God every day for answering what I thought was an impossible prayer.

— *Father John T. Catoir*

THE CHRISTOPHERS

Father James Keller, M.M., founded The Christophers in 1945 to promote the idea that God has a special task in life for each person, that you can make a difference in this world, and that positive action can work miracles. Over the years, The Christophers have produced radio and television programs, books, pamphlets, and youth programs designed to promote their message. Their motto is: "It's better to light one candle than to curse the darkness."

I Asked God to Guide Me

I drifted away from the Catholic Church in high school. When I got to university, I became involved with Campus Crusade for

Christ. I had initially returned to the Catholic Church, but my mentor was an ex-Catholic, who was fairly anti-Catholic, and he convinced me to walk away.

I started bouncing around different churches and non-denominational campus groups. At one point, I ran into a friend who was working on his Master of Business Administration degree. He was a Mormon. When he found out I was bouncing around, he asked if I would do a Bible study with him. I ended up meeting with him and two other men, who, I later found out, were Mormon missionaries. Towards the end of the Bible study, they wanted me to make a commitment to becoming a Mormon. Their arguments made a lot of sense. The way they used scriptures and the Book of Mormon was very convincing — especially for a young man like myself who was struggling to figure out life.

The day before they wanted a decision, I was reading and praying. I asked God to guide me. Then I flipped open my Bible and read: "And I solemnly declare to everyone who hears the words of prophecy written in this book: If anyone adds anything to what is written here, God will add to that person the plagues described in this book. And if anyone removes any of the words from this book of prophecy, God will remove that person's share in the tree of life and in the holy city that are described in this book" (Revelation 22:18–19).

I called my Mormon friends and canceled the Bible study for the next day. I went to confession and Mass. It took months to get them to stop calling me, but I just kept going to daily Mass to grow my faith. This is my story of answered prayer, but also my story of returning to the Catholic faith.

— *Steven R. McEvoy*

HOW TO GO TO CONFESSION

Catholics who have not received the Sacrament of Reconciliation in a while sometimes worry about what to say and do. Most people start with the words, "Bless me, Father, for I have sinned" and then estimate how long it has been since their last confession. No priest will expect you to remember every sin you have committed since your last confession. Some will help you through a general examination of conscience. Others might ask if there is a particular sin that you want to mention. When you have finished, the priest will ask you to express sorrow for your sins using your own words or by praying an Act of Contrition. If you are not sure what to say, don't worry. The priest will help you. He will give you some penance to perform — usually prayers, a work of mercy, or an act of charity. Then you will receive absolution and a blessing.

I Can't Do This Anymore

My faith journey started when I met my future wife. I was raised Methodist, but I never got confirmed. I wasn't into faith. Anna's parents were traditional Italian Catholics. When Anna and I were getting engaged, her parents said, "He's got to be Catholic if you are going to get married."

I said sure. It wasn't a big deal for me.

So I became a Catholic, and then the kids were baptized. We would go to Mass. But I was still very secular. I was still struggling with a lot of things. I had started a new company, and I was working sixteen-hour days. Everything was about work and money for me. Anna and I were struggling in our marriage. It was getting to be too much.

Then one day, when I was driving home, I prayed, "God, I can't do this anymore. I am trying to control everything. I just can't do this by myself. I give it up to you, God. I give the company up to you. If you want it to succeed, it will succeed. I am going to do the best I can, but I am going to stop and trust you."

After that, everything in my life started to turn around. The company started making money. Our married life got better. My relationship with the kids got better. Letting go of control was a huge moment for me. Now I trust whatever God wants, and I let it flow from there.

— *Mike Nuzzo*

LETTING GO

Many people operate under the illusion that they have control over their lives. Letting go does not mean that you stop caring about what happens in your life. It means that you empty yourself of everything that is not important and then use the time and energy you formerly spent trying to control everything in a more positive direction toward things that are really important. In the process, you free yourself from a lot of useless stress and anxiety. Letting go is really about learning to trust God. It's not always easy — especially if you have a long habit of trying to maintain control. You may find that you have to consciously let go every day for the rest of your life — and that's okay.

God Had Other Plans

In the '90s, there was much unrest in the Los Angeles area, and I was feeling more and more uncomfortable living there. Some friends and family members had moved to Oregon. I decided that maybe it was time for me to move, too. But where? I asked God to guide me, but of course I had my own ideas.

The first logical spot was Oregon. I sent out numerous résumés, and I didn't receive even one reply.

A family member asked, "If you could live anywhere in the country, where would it be?" I am not a "hot and humid" weather person, and I rather love snow and mountains, so the northern part of the U.S. seemed logical. I had been to Colorado and Utah and knew of their beauty. And even though I hadn't seen it, Vermont was also on my list.

Before I had a chance to send out résumés to these other states, I talked with friends who said, "Why don't you try Wisconsin?"

Now, I had only been to Wisconsin once. The area I saw was pretty flat, and I wasn't impressed. But I long ago learned that when God puts something in front of you, you see where it leads. So I sent out a number of résumés, expecting the same results as with those sent to Oregon. But, surprise! This time I heard from everyone! Whether or not they had a position, they answered my inquiries.

So, in the spring, I went to Wisconsin to "check things out." I secretly figured that this trip would eliminate Wisconsin from the list. But God had other plans. Within that one week, I accepted three part-time positions, and I found a house that was situated in a town right in the middle of the three jobs. Plus, it was only about a half-hour from my friends.

For many years now I have called the "Hidden Gem of Wisconsin" my home and have thanked God every day that I was open to his guidance to receive such a very special and surprising answer to my prayers. It is a gift that has included wonderful friends, a strong sense of community, and positions in my field and in the Catholic Church that I never dreamed of having.

— *Helen A. Scieszka, Ph.D.*

PRAYER OF ENTRUSTMENT

When we need to turn a situation over to God, Pope Francis recommends this Prayer of Entrustment: "Lord, I entrust this to you; you help take care of it."

"It is a beautiful Christian prayer," Pope Francis explains. "It is the attitude of trust in the power of the Lord, and in the tenderness of God who is Father."

Lord, Help Me!

A guy I was working with asked me to go to New York City with him to pick up a car. We took a bus, and we got in at midnight. He grew up in New York City, so he knew where he was going. We got on the subway. The train was crowded. Then my friend got off at a stop, and I couldn't get off in time. The doors closed, and I was still on the train. I prayed, "Lord help me!"

The train came up from underground, and I got off at the next station. I didn't know what to do. So I jumped down on the track and ran toward the last station. I stayed on the tracks into the tunnel and went underground. Luckily for me there was no other train coming. Up ahead, I saw my friend, Joe, on the platform with about twenty other people. They were screaming at me, "Climb on the platform!" So I did. Joe pointed down at the track and told me that if I had stepped on the third rail, I would have been electrocuted.

I had run along that whole track, and I never touched the third rail. The Lord was there every step of the way for me.

— *Mark Piscitello*

CHAPTER 11

To Forgive and to Be Forgiven

Prayer and forgiveness are inseparable. Every time we pray an Our Father, we ask God to forgive us for all of the ways we have hurt others, and we acknowledge to God that we are willing to forgive those who have hurt us (Matthew 6:12).

The Gospel doesn't leave any room for doubt when it comes to forgiveness. Jesus tells us to forgive our enemies (Matthew 5:44). When Peter asks if it is enough to forgive seven times, Jesus tells him to forgive seventy times seven times (Matthew 18:22). On the cross, Jesus gives us the ultimate example of forgiveness when he prays, "Father, forgive them; for they know not what they do" (Luke 23:34).

Pope Francis points out that there is another aspect of forgiveness that is often overlooked. "*Forgiveness* is, above all, what we ourselves receive from God," he says. "Only the awareness that we are sinners forgiven by God's infinite mercy can enable us to carry out concrete gestures of fraternal reconciliation. If a person does not feel that he/she is a sinner who has been forgiven, that person will never be able to make a gesture of forgiveness or reconciliation."

When we forgive, we make a conscious decision to let go of the hurt. It doesn't matter whether we're right or wrong. It doesn't matter whether the other person wants or deserves our forgiveness. We forgive because forgiveness frees us from anger, resentment, frustration, and thoughts of revenge. It restores spiritual, mental, and emotional wholeness. Without forgiveness, bitterness takes control of our lives. It hardens our hearts. It affects our prayer life, our relationships, our thought processes, and our health.

Forgiveness is good for us, but it is not always easy. Some people struggle with deep childhood wounds that can involve anger, violence, abuse, or feelings of abandonment. Other people wrestle with hurt feelings, misunderstandings, and mistakes that result in broken relationships. Sometimes it is a tremendous struggle to forgive ourselves for things we are ashamed of doing. Sometimes, no matter what we say or do, the people we have hurt will not forgive us.

Our only hope of seeking forgiveness, forgiving others, and forgiving ourselves is to allow God to enter into our pain and transform our lives in ways we never thought possible. The stories in this chapter illustrate some of the ways people have learned how to forgive and to be forgiven.

HOW TO FORGIVE

Forgiveness requires prayer, persistence, and patience:

- Begin by asking God for the generosity to forgive as he forgives.
- Write about it. Then burn the paper and let the smoke become a symbol of giving it to God.
- Reflect on Jesus' words from the Sermon on the Mount: "Love your enemies and pray for those who persecute you" (Matthew 5:44).
- Talk to a priest or go to confession and say, "I've been angry and hurt for a long time, and I want to let go of this."
- Pray for the person who caused the hurt.

- Ask God's forgiveness for the ways you've hurt others.
- If anger resurfaces, remind yourself that you have already made the decision to forgive. Ask God to keep you from slipping back into bitterness or resentment.

Forgiving My Mother and Myself

From the time I was a little girl, my mother told me that she did not want to be pregnant when I was conceived and born. I felt so guilty and, unconsciously, I blamed myself, as if I had somehow caused her pain.

I tried to make it up to her for all the ways I had hurt her. I was a good girl, but never good enough. I tried to make her proud of me and to make her love me the way I thought I needed to be loved, but it didn't happen. This one wound left me with a gaping hole that just couldn't be filled. I dragged around the weight of this wound for a long, long time.

It wasn't until many years later when I was praying with Scripture that I read the passage, "You shall love the Lord your God with all your heart, and with all your soul, and with all your mind.... You shall love your neighbor as yourself" (Matthew 22:37, 39). The words touched a raw nerve! Love my neighbor as myself? It never occurred to me to love myself. I had always thought that loving myself was selfish, but I was wrong. I had to learn to love myself.

In the process, I learned to surrender to the Lord what was not in my grasp to change or control. I learned that the only person I could change or control is myself — with the help of the Lord. I learned that forgiving myself and my mother was vital to my coming to know our loving and merciful God.

As I surrendered my childhood wounds to the Lord, I began to see my mother in the light of her own wounds. I started to pray for her daily. I no longer took on any negatives that she tossed my way. I saw her as lonely and afraid. I began to think that maybe she never experienced the love of God. Over time, my childhood wounds turned to gratitude and thanksgiving because, without those wounds, I might not have learned how to love God, my neighbor, and myself.

— *Kathleen Skipper*

HEALING THE PAIN OF THE PAST

Painful memories of an accusing, punishing, or unloving parent can trigger a host of self-defeating emotions in us as adults. You can't deny what happened in the past, but you don't have to let what happened in the past dominate your life. The first step to healing the pain of the past is to consciously turn off the negative messages that you internalized as a child. Then override those bad messages with positive messages that are grounded in truth: "I am not a bad person. God loves me. God cares about me. God will never abandon me."

Healing does not happen instantly. It is a process that carries you to a deep understanding that you are lovable because you are loved by God.

"Real love is about loving and letting yourself be loved," Pope Francis explains. "It's harder to let yourself be loved than to love. That is why it is so difficult to come to the perfect love of God. We can love him but we must let ourselves be loved by him. Real love is being open to the love that comes to you."

Bearing Wrongs Patiently

I have a good friend, who I have known since she was ten years old. We worked together, and her oldest boy is my godson. About two years ago, I said something that was misinterpreted, and it abruptly ended our friendship.

Lately, I have been praying for two things relative to the spiritual works of mercy. The first is forgiveness, and the second is to bear wrongs patiently. I felt like I have not been forgiven, and I have been praying for that forgiveness. I have also been praying that I could bear this patiently.

Then suddenly, there was a breakthrough. My friend's younger son graduated from high school, so I called and asked if I could send him a graduation gift. She said that would be okay. So I sent a gift, and a few weeks later I received a wonderful thank-you note from him saying how important I had been in his life. Then he sent me an invitation to his graduation party.

I called and left a voicemail message for his mom: "I would love to come and see him, but I don't want to cause any angst. So I respectfully decline."

I didn't hear anything for another week, and then, the day before the party, she called and left a voicemail message saying, "It would mean a lot to him if you came."

Everyone at the party was very gracious, but I didn't spend any time talking to my old friend. I talked to both boys. Then, at the end, when I said good-bye, she hugged me. She said she wanted me to start coming to the boys' soccer games. She said, "The past is past."

It was a huge burden off me, and I know it was an answer to my prayer.

— Joe Smyth

SEEKING FORGIVENESS

Seeking forgiveness requires prayer, introspection, and humility:

- Begin by deeply reflecting on how you hurt this person, why you acted in the way that you did, and how you would feel if someone did this to you.
- Pray that God will help you make this right.
- Ask God to forgive you for any wrongs you have committed.
- With great humility, sincerely ask the person who is hurt to forgive you.
- Even if your actions were unintentional or misinterpreted, acknowledge that this person feels upset or wounded.
- Accept whatever situation unfolds. Be grateful if the person forgives you. Be understanding if the person is not ready to let this go.
- Continue to pray for this person and for yourself.

A Prayer of Trust and Thankfulness

I am a staff member of Madonna House, an apostolate of lay men, women, and priests, who serve the needs of the poor in our field houses around the world. While I was assigned to our field house in Moncton, New Brunswick, my folks announced that they were coming from Chicago for a visit. My relationship with my dad was not easy. We often reacted to one another in negative ways, so I was apprehensive.

This was a small field house, just two staff members. We started to pray by thanking God for what he would do while my folks were with us. We did this for about a month. Then my folks came. We thought they would come for a weekend, then travel the Maritimes, and stay with us another weekend on their way home. They spent *ONE MONTH* with us! In the mornings, they did their own thing, and in the afternoons they worked with us at Madonna House.

On the one side trip they took, I went with them. We traveled to Cape Breton. It was a very demanding trip, with the brake shoe linings of their RV burning out. Tensions ran high. I was very mean to Dad at one point — and then I was so disappointed in myself.

But I didn't have to reach to the depths of my being to start over, to forgive him, and to forgive myself. Because of all that prayer during the month before, I knew that Jesus was there, holding me up. I was able to ask forgiveness, give forgiveness, and move on. It was remarkable, and the experience taught me about the power of praying before an event. It was the prayers of thanksgiving for what would happen when my folks arrived — which were prayers of both trust and thankfulness.

And God came through!

— *Bonnie Staib*

WHAT IS MADONNA HOUSE?

Madonna House is a community of lay men, women, and priests who strive to love and serve Jesus Christ in all aspects of life. Founded in 1947 by Catherine de Hueck Doherty, in Combermere, Ontario, Madonna House has missionary field houses worldwide.

My Unforgivable Sin

I was sexually abused at age eleven, and I thought that because I had not stopped the abuse, I had committed an unforgiveable sin. My spiritual director told me that if I really wanted to get over this, there was something I could do. He put me under obedience to spend an hour in prayer every day. He warned it may take a while before something changed, and he was right.

The first couple of weeks, I tried to open up my heart to the love of God. But as soon as I did, I could feel my heart slamming shut. So, for two years, I just sat in the chapel every day with my arms folded, and I dared God to do something. Then during the homily at Mass one Sunday, the priest said, "What God does is this: once we confess our sins, once he has forgiven them, he sees them as stepping stones that become a pathway that leads us to him."

I don't remember the rest of the homily, and I don't remember the rest of the Mass. I just sat there, and an image of myself as a little boy came to mind. This little boy was in a pit surrounded by a wall of stones, but suddenly the stones fell back, making a staircase. These stairs were a pathway that would lead me to God!

Suddenly I knew that God's love is stronger than my sense of sinfulness. God's love is what kept me sitting in that chapel until I reached a place where I could open my heart. But the really great grace in all this is that now I am able to sit in the chapel and open my heart, knowing that God's love is stronger than anything in my life. Would all of this have happened if I had not been faithful to that one hour of prayer a day? Somehow, I don't think so.

— *Peter Gravelle*

Forgiving the Woman Who Killed Our Son

On November 1, 2014, our seventeen-year-old son, Dominik, was returning from a Halloween party with friends when their car ran out of gas on the Beltway around Washington, D.C. The boys were waiting for help when an oncoming vehicle veered onto the shoulder of the road and crashed into them. Dominik, who was sitting in the back seat, died instantly.

Our family has always had a deep devotion to Divine Mercy. When our children were little, we traveled to Poland several times where we prayed at the tomb of Saint Faustina. There was never any doubt in our minds that it was the merciful Jesus who was carrying us through the devastating death of Dominik. And we came to believe that through Dominik's death, others would experience Divine Mercy.

Our parish was too small to handle a large funeral, so arrangements were made for Dominik's funeral to be held at the National Shrine of the Immaculate Conception, the largest Catholic church in North America. The Divine Mercy image was placed in front of the ambo, and we asked that the Rosary and the Divine Mercy Chaplet be prayed before Mass. On one side of Dominik's memorial card was the Divine Mercy image and on the other side was how to pray the Divine Mercy Chaplet.

After the Mass, a family member read a statement in which we expressed our deep sorrow, but also our belief that God would not have taken Dominik unless he had a mission for him. We asked each person in the standing-room-only basilica to practice active mercy and kindness toward one another, to share with the world that we have an all-merciful God, and to believe that no sin is too great that it cannot be forgiven.

In the months that followed, small miracles began to unfold. Several people had dreams about Dominik. Some told us how they felt Dominik's presence. Others said Dominik and the message of mercy had renewed their faith and changed their lives. It changed our lives, as well.

Because of our devotion to Divine Mercy we wanted to forgive the woman who killed our son. We called her the day before Dominik's funeral to see how she was doing. In the months that followed, we continued to pray for her. We met with her in person eleven months after the accident. She told us that she was suffering, too, and how much our forgiveness has helped her.

When you don't forgive, you hold on to anger, and it only hurts you more. You can't be free. Our faith in Divine Mercy helped us to forgive — even though we still feel the loss and the sadness of losing our son. But God gives us the grace we need, and when we are open, more graces come to us. It is the answer to our prayers.

— *Magdalena and Patrick Pettey*

DIVINE MERCY

Devotion to Jesus as Divine Mercy flows from the diaries of Saint Faustina. The message of Divine Mercy is based on the simple truth that God loves us, and that his mercy is greater than any sin we may commit. Because of this, we are called to trust Jesus, accept his mercy, and become instruments of his mercy by extending love and forgiveness to others. The Divine Mercy Chaplet is a prayer that was composed from the writings of Saint Faustina.

CHAPTER 12

Money from Heaven

People often wonder if it is okay to pray for money. The answer to that question depends on why you are seeking financial help. If the reason is to build personal wealth, then the answer is a resounding no! We see that played out in the Gospel of Luke, when someone asks Jesus to tell a family member to share the inheritance. Jesus refuses. Then Jesus warns, "Take heed, and beware of all covetousness; for a man's life does not consist in the abundance of his possessions" (Luke 12:15).

But what if you are praying for a legitimate need or to help someone else in need — even if it is one of your own family members? In those instances, the Lord will hear your cry for assistance. "He will regard the prayer of the destitute, and will not despise their supplication" (Psalm 102:17). But here must also be an attitude of faith and trust in the Lord. Jesus told his disciples not to worry about where food and clothing will come from. He used the example of birds, who have no storehouses or barns but are fed by God. "Of how much more value are you than the birds!" (Luke 12:24).

Reflecting on the Gospel passage about the multiplication of the loaves and fishes, Pope Francis points out that the people who had gathered to listen to Jesus were tired and hungry. The disciples looked at them from a human point of view. They wanted to dismiss the crowd so that the people could go into the village and find food. "Jesus' outlook is very different," Pope Francis observes. "It is dictated by his union with the Father and his compassion for the people, that mercifulness of Jesus for us all. Jesus senses our problems, he senses our weaknesses, he senses our needs."

When we recognize that everything we have is a gift from God, and we strive to use those gifts to serve God, to help other people, and to make the world a better place, then we are good stewards. In their pastoral letter on stewardship, the Catholic bishops in the United States explained that a good steward is someone who "receives God's gifts gratefully, cherishes and tends them in a responsible and accountable manner, shares them in justice and love with others, and returns them with increase to the Lord."

This chapter highlights the different ways God listens and responds to good stewards who came to him with strong faith and authentic financial need.

WHEN MONEY BECOMES AN IDOL

Pope Francis has warned against making money an idol. "Money is important, especially when there is none, and food, school, and the children's future depend on it," he explained. "But it becomes an idol when it becomes the aim. Greed, which by no coincidence is a capital sin, is the sin of idolatry because the accumulation of money per se becomes the aim of one's own actions. It was precisely Jesus who defined money as 'lord': 'No one can serve two lords, two masters.' . . . The best and most practical way to avoid making an idol of money is to share it, share it with others, above all with the poor, or to enable young people to study and work.... When you share and donate your profits, you are performing an act of lofty spirituality, saying to money through deeds: 'you are not God, you are not lord, you are not master!' "

The Lord Takes Care of Everything

In the early days, when we were starting our inner-city mission, we were in debt. We needed $25,000. I went to Adoration, and I told the Lord I needed the money to continue helping his people. I felt as if the Lord was telling me that first I had to forgive everyone who ever offended me.

So I went through my whole life and forgave everyone. That was on a Monday. The following Saturday, the mail came. The first envelope had a check for $25.00. The second envelope had a check for $100. The third envelope had a check for $25,000. The letter said that the donor had come down to see what we were doing at the mission and was sending us the check "in the name of Jesus Christ." That's how the letter was signed. The Lord saved St. Luke's.

The Lord makes sure we have everything we need to help his people. One time in the early days, the kitchen was running out of food to serve the one hundred people who depended on us for daily meals. The volunteers were in a panic, but the woman in charge of the kitchen said, "Let's pray to the Lord that we don't ever run out of food!" So they prayed, and the next day a man showed up with ten cases of ham. Then another truck came with potatoes, carrots, and other produce. Another truck came with butter. St. Luke's never ran out of food again.

The Lord always answers as long as we are doing his will. An observer came to the mission one day and remarked about how poor we are. One of the children overheard and said to me, "Are we poor?"

I told him, "No, we are rich, because the Lord takes care of everything we need."

— Amy Betros
St. Luke's Mission of Mercy

RELYING ON DIVINE PROVIDENCE

Because they place all of their trust in God's Divine Providence, St. Luke's Mission of Mercy does not accept money from the government or the diocese. The ministry operates on donations from individuals, organizations, and businesses that are willing to share with those who are in need.

"I Don't Know Where This Money Will Come From"

My husband, Jack, was working on his degree in social work, and I was the breadwinner of the family. I didn't make a lot of money. When I got home one night, there were two bills — a tax bill and a tuition bill for Jack. I was so exhausted. I couldn't do one more thing. So I knelt down and I prayed, "Dear God, we need $1,000. I don't know where this money will come from, but I am so grateful that you do."

The next day the director of the agency where Jack was doing his field work called him in and said, "I was thinking it must be pretty tough for you going through this program with four kids at home. I have the discretion to give out a stipend. So I want you to stop at the office on your way out and pick up an envelope." The envelope had a check for $1,000.

— *F. de Sales Kellick*

We Don't Pray for Money

As members of the St. Vincent de Paul Society, we start all of our meetings with prayer and end with a prayer. We don't pray for money. We pray for guidance in seeking and finding the deprived so we can give them the love of God.

About five or six years ago, Catholic Charities told us they were having budget problems and they could no longer give us the $80,000 subsidy we needed for our summer camp program for poor children. We understood, but it was a shock, and the timing was not good because we had already started accepting registrations for the summer camp.

A few years before, there was a disabled elderly lady at one of the parishes who was kind of cranky. The parishioners who were taking Holy Communion to her told the pastor that they didn't want to visit her anymore. The pastor called us and asked if St. Vincent de Paul members could take over. For several years, our members visited her on a regular basis. Then she passed away and left the St. Vincent de Paul Society her home and all of its contents. The check from her estate was $80,000, and it came to us just at the time we needed it for the summer camp!

Stories like this happen not only to us, but to a lot of St. Vincent de Paul conferences. All of a sudden there will be a need for something and we don't have the resources. The next thing you know, we've got it!

—*Jim Byron*

SOCIETY OF ST. VINCENT DE PAUL

In 1833, twenty-year-old Frédéric Ozanam was so disturbed by the poverty he witnessed on the streets of Paris that he organized fellow students, who begged for money, fuel, food, and clothing that they could distribute to the poor. Ozanam assured his followers: "I am now completely convinced that when one does a deed of charity one need not worry about where the money will come from: it will always come."

The students met weekly. They chose as their patron Saint Vincent de Paul (1581–1660), a French priest who had dedicated his life to serving the poor. Ozanam's group of students grew rapidly to more than 600 members, and it wasn't long before fifteen additional groups were organized in neighboring cities and towns. By 1845, Conferences of Charity under the patronage of Saint Vincent de Paul had been established throughout Europe and were spreading to the United States and Mexico. Today, the St. Vincent de Paul Society can be found in 142 countries, with over one million members whose mission is to "seek and find the forgotten, the suffering, or the deprived."

Frédéric Ozanam died in 1853. He was beatified by Pope John Paul II in 1997.

"God Has Money"

In 2014, I found myself face-to-face with what seemed like an impossible challenge: I had been accepted as an aspirant to a religious community, but in order to become a postulant I had to pay off $25,000 in student loan debt … in three months. The sisters kept reassuring me that if God really wanted me there, everything would work out. "God has money," the vocation director reminded me more than once. "He has all the money."

In my head, I believed that, but my heart just could not seem to accept it. I spent weeks on a roller coaster of emotions, swinging from moments of peace and acceptance of God's will to hours in the grip of anxiety. What if I couldn't get the loans paid down? What if I couldn't enter the convent that summer? What if … what if…? I told myself I was open to God's will, but in reality I was terrified that his will and mine wouldn't line up. What then?

Through the application process, I had also run into some medical issues I had not been aware of before. The diagnostic screenings and resulting medications cost money, further compounding my stress. Things took a turn for the worse the day I discovered a bill for yet another screening. Apparently, my insurance would only cover so much, and I owed nearly $800. Worn out with praying about money, I put the bill back in its envelope, laid it on the table, and said aloud, "Well, Lord, this one's on you." Oddly enough, after that I felt an enormous sense of peace. In fact, I forgot all about the bill and my money worries for several days.

About two weeks later, a mysterious envelope showed up in my pile of mail. I held my breath as I opened it, assuming it would be yet another medical bill. I almost fell over in my surprise at what I found instead: a check in my name, for almost the exact amount I owed for my medical screening. To this day, I'm not really sure where that money came from, but I do know it was an answer to my prayer. Over the next two months, I also received all the help I needed (and more) to cover my remaining student loans. As a result, I was blessed to spend two wonderful years in religious life, before discerning God's call to lay life. And I learned that God always provides — we truly do not need to worry about anything.

— *Mary Beth Baker*

"You Have to Help Us!"

I was the coordinator of a parish outreach program that sponsored a food pantry in an economically depressed area of Buffalo, New York. When the parish told me they could no longer support the program financially, I went to the six other parishes in the area to ask for their support. Since the food pantry was serving all of the people in the community, I also approached the Lutheran Evangelical Church, the Russian Orthodox Church, the United Church of Christ, and the Baptist Church.

Everyone told me that they appreciated the work of the outreach program. They all recognized the need. They were happy to recruit volunteers for us, but none of the churches could provide financial support because they were all facing financial difficulties. Even Catholic Charities said they could not afford to sponsor the program.

I wrote a letter to the bishop explaining the situation, and I asked for his help, but I did not receive an answer. I found out later he sent my letter to Catholic Charities.

In desperation, I turned to God. I said: "Look, Lord, in Matthew 25:35–40, you said, 'I was hungry and you gave me food....' That's what we're trying to do in this outreach program. Nobody has any money to support the food pantry. I have done everything I can, and no one can help me! These are your people who need help. You have to help us!"

A short time later Catholic Charities called. They had just learned of a new initiative from the Robert Wood Johnson Foundation, which wanted to support an ecumenical outreach program! After applying for the grant, we were awarded $25,000. My prayer was answered, and a new interfaith ministry was born.

Nothing is impossible with God!

— *Sister Rose Therese DiGregorio, O.S.F.*

Jesus Answers — Even When We Whine

I was whining to my spiritual director, Sister Nancy, about family finances *AGAIN*. "Whenever I ask the Lord for money we need, I get no answer," I complained.

Sister Nancy stopped me in mid-sentence. "Do you remember a few years ago when you asked Jesus to help the last of your children with the money for college? And didn't all five of your children receive scholarships for the colleges of their choice? Did you ever add up all the financial aid they received?"

"No," I replied sheepishly.

Sister Nancy handed me paper and a pen to start a tally. After a few minutes, I had figures next to each child's name. Then came the moment of revelation: their scholarships and other financial aid totaled over $500,000.

Sister Nancy took the list and whispered, "Your prayers have been answered!"

— *John Boucher*

CHAPTER 13

Without a Doubt

There are times when we pray for something specific, and afterward there is no doubt in our minds that God has answered our prayer. Sometimes, the revelation of answered prayer comes instantly or within a very short period of time. The realization can be overwhelming when we see how God has responded. The experience strengthens our faith and our trust in God. We feel as if we have been blessed in a special way.

Other times, it is only in hindsight that we realize the way in which our prayer has been answered. There's an old saying that God writes straight with crooked lines. Sometimes, the answer to our prayers takes a strange route through many twists and turns in life.

In some instances, a delayed answer to prayer takes so long that we have already forgotten about our initial request. Or maybe we gave up praying because we assumed our prayer was never going to be answered. When the answer finally comes, we can usually see, through the eyes of faith, the wisdom of God in delaying his response. We see that we may not have been ready for the answer sooner, or we see that other circumstances had to unfold before we could fully appreciate the answer to our prayer.

Every time a prayer is answered, the best response is one of gratitude to God for giving us the answer we hoped to receive, gratitude to God for waiting until we were ready to receive the answer, or gratitude to God for loving us enough to give us what is best.

Pope Francis tells us that we must never forget the extraordinary ways God has worked in our lives. "We must look back and remember and do it often. 'At that time God gave me this grace and I replied in that way, I did this or that … he accompanied me.' And in this way we arrive at a new encounter, an encounter of gratitude."

The stories in this chapter show some of the different ways that people received confirmation that their prayer had been answered, and how those answered prayers impacted their lives and the lives of people around them.

"This Lady Can Go In"

When my son was a senior in college, he developed chronic fatigue syndrome, a complicated disorder with extreme fatigue that can worsen with physical or mental activity and does not improve with rest. We were told in prayer that he would be healed, but in the meantime, he was unable to return to school.

While he was still at home, the newspaper did an article about the families of two teenagers who had been convicted for robbing and murdering two local priests several years prior. My son was so incensed that the newspaper would again expose these families that he decided to write a letter to one of the teenagers who was serving life in prison. Milton wrote back, and they began a correspondence. After a while, my son started to visit Milton. During their visits, they talked about their families. Before long, Milton, who had a horrible family life, expressed an interest in meeting me.

I wasn't sure that I wanted to meet him. Our pastor was close friends with one of the murdered priests. After the incident, I had started praying for the perpetrators, the families of the priests, and our pastor. Never did I think that those prayers would lead to my meeting one of the teenagers. I started praying for an answer as to whether I should visit.

I had not yet received a clear answer to my prayer, but I knew that my son really wanted me to go, so I finally agreed. The two of us started to visit Milton every few weeks. But I kept asking the Lord, "Is this really what you want me to do?"

The answer came one day when we got to the prison. I realized that I didn't have my photo ID, which you need in order to get inside. As we inched our way toward the guards at the desk, I said to my son, "I'm not going to get in, so I will go and wait in the car."

Just then, I heard this woman's voice saying, "Hi, Mrs. McLean! You had me in eighth-grade religion class, and I wasn't very nice to you!"

I didn't really remember this young woman, but we had a warm exchange. She told me about herself and her family. She was now a commanding officer at the prison. By this point, my son and I were almost to the guard's desk, and I told her I was going to have to go back to the car because I forgot my photo ID. She said to the guard, "This lady can go in. She is who she says she is!"

Sometimes the Lord has to hit me over the head to get me to hear what he's telling me. This was like a real clunk on the head to let me know that visiting Milton at the prison was what the Lord wanted me to do.

— *Carolyn McLean*

There's My Answer!

My wife's cousin has leukemia. He is really sick. I wanted to share with him the Divine Mercy Chaplet, but it didn't seem like an opportune time. I told the Lord that I would leave it in his hands.

Listening to Catholic radio the next morning, a priest said, "Sometimes you can't preach Jesus right away. It's all in the Lord's time. Sometimes we just have to accept people where they are at."

There was my answer! I said, "Okay, Lord, it's in your hands. I'll pray, hope, and trust in you."

— *Mark Piscitello*

The House I Prayed For

A few years ago, a woman suggested that I buy her mother's house. While it sounded like a house I had wanted many years ago, I was happy where I was living, and felt I was too old to go through purchasing a new house and moving.

After a few days, I found myself imagining that I was celebrating Christmas in that house. I called the real estate agent and went to see the house, thinking it would get it out of my mind. That didn't work. So I took my son and then my brother to see the house. I expected both of them to tell me why I shouldn't buy the house, but they both thought it was "my house."

I began to figure out how to pay for a new house, and every step I took brought me to the next step. I made an offer on the house, and it was accepted! The financing fell into place. Thirty days after I first looked at the house, I was the proud owner. I moved in and began to use the house for Bible study, RCIA sessions, and a prayer-shawl ministry. The house also became a place for family and friends to gather.

I was telling someone how it was very like a house I had prayed for when I was young because I wanted a house big enough for when my parents and siblings came to visit. I was so shocked because in that moment I realized that God had answered my prayer. God knew that I needed forty years to elapse before I could appreciate and afford this house.

— *Susan Stout*

God and I Agreed!

Many years ago, as part of my personal and spiritual growth, the idea of finding a spiritual director was brought to my attention. So I shared with a number of people, as well as God, that "I" wanted a male, preferably a priest who was at the very least "like a Jesuit." Plus, "I" thought it would be a good idea that he had some education or background in counseling.

Within a week, two different sources that were in no way connected to each other brought me the same name … Father Leo Rock, S.J., Ph.D.! Not only was he a priest, but he was also a Jesuit and a psychologist.

It is one of the few times that God and I agreed on what was best for me, and I am very grateful. This man touched and changed my life in so many wonderful ways. I was forever blessed.

— *Helen A. Scieszka, Ph.D.*

WHAT IS A SPIRITUAL DIRECTOR?

A spiritual director is a priest, a nun, or a layperson who has been trained to listen and help discern the movement of the Holy Spirit in another person's life. Spiritual direction has been an important part of Catholic tradition for centuries, but only recently have increasing numbers of laypeople discovered that spiritual direction is a good way to grow closer to God.

A Good Mother

My mother tells the story of when she was still single and she prayed that if she ever had children God would let her know that she was a good mother by letting one of her children become a priest or a nun. So, when I told her I was going to join the Companions of the Cross, she cried because she saw that God answered her prayer and was saying that she had done a good job as a mother!

— *Father John Fletcher, C.C.*

PRAYER FOR VOCATIONS

Gracious and Loving God, send down your grace upon the men and women who are discerning a vocation to priesthood and religious life. Help them to hear and answer your call. Fill them with your love. Instill in them a deep desire to serve others. Allow them to see that they will find meaning and purpose in making a lifelong commitment to you. Give them the courage they need to surrender themselves to your holy will. Bestow upon them the peace that the world cannot give. We ask this through Jesus Christ, our Lord. Amen.

Trusting in God's Plan

I was pregnant with my first child when I suddenly experienced tremendous abdominal pain. My husband rushed me to the emergency room. The nurses assumed that I was "just miscarrying" and wanted to send me home. But my pain was so intense that my husband refused to leave. After that, the medical staff showed no interest in helping me. I was literally screaming in pain.

Two hours later, I looked my husband in the eyes and said, "John, I'm dying. I feel my kidneys shutting down. We need to pray." I moaned as John prayed the Our Father, Hail Mary, and Glory Be. I was terrified, and all I could do was put everything in God's hands.

A short time after we started praying, the doctor on call came to see me. He ordered an ultrasound that showed I had an interstitial pregnancy, which happens when the baby implants where the fallopian tube and the uterus meet. As the baby grew, both the tube and my uterus suddenly ruptured causing massive internal bleeding.

Things happened quickly after the ultrasound. The burning in my kidneys went away, but my blood pressure dropped to 40/50. Everything went warm and floaty. The last thing I felt was John's hand moving mine to sign consent for surgery and the fluttering of the nurses' hands as they removed my jewelry.

Our prayers saved my life. God heard us, and he sent the doctor who saved me. We named the baby I miscarried that night Angelica, messenger of God.

After our loss, I prayed directly to Jesus to heal my womb for future babies. Two months later, we conceived our daughter Adelaide. I was told by doctors that I could not carry a baby beyond thirty-seven weeks without re-rupturing my uterus, yet I carried Adelaide to thirty-seven weeks and five days.

During my next pregnancy, I prayed fervently, asking God to guide me. I wanted to attempt a natural birth instead of a cesarean. That's when my daughter Adelaide got one of those free Gideon Bibles from the fair. It was open to 2 Timothy 1:1–13. I read the passage, and I knew then that God was telling me to trust in him.

Unfortunately, I ended up having an emergency cesarean because of pre-eclampsia. But I felt that, through my prayers, I was guided by the Holy Spirit to trust in God's will. I felt the

Holy Spirit so strongly that I named the baby Eunice, from the Scripture passage that encouraged me to trust God. The name Eunice means "a glorious victory." The name fitted her perfectly, considering how victorious I felt with my spiritual victory in trusting God's will and my physical victory in carrying Eunice to thirty-nine weeks and three days.

Now I trust in God's plan. My path has unfolded, and I rely on my own experiences when I speak to other moms about loss. I try to bring them comfort by listening, validating, and offering them hope.

— *Sarah Teresa Belanger*

The Pain Stopped at 5:00 p.m.

Several years ago my sister-in-law, who was a prayer-team member, suffered a heart attack. As they were taking her to the ambulance, she told a neighbor to get on her computer and email me an emergency prayer request for the prayer team.

I sent the prayer request out immediately. When Fran came home from the hospital, she told me that she knew what time the emergency prayer request went out because her pain stopped at exactly 5:00 p.m. I went to my computer, and she was right! The emergency prayer request was sent to the team members at exactly 5:00 p.m.

— *Nancy Riecke*

WHAT IS A PRAYER TEAM?

Many parishes have organized a group of people who are willing to pray for the intentions of others. These groups are sometimes called prayer chains, prayer lines, or prayer ministries. People can call or email the person in charge of the prayer team with special intentions, and the members of the prayer team are then contacted.

A Lesson in Faith and Patience

In January 1995, I was working as the editorial director for Servant Publications. That month we sold a remarkable ten thousand copies of a devotional by Pope John Paul II. I told the publishing team that we should immediately bring out another book by the pope that would piggyback on our success. "We should do a book called *Breakfast with the Pope*," I suggested. The team thought I was joking and pooh-poohed the idea.

I let it go. But over the next month, I became convinced that the idea was sound. At the February meeting, I told the team I wanted us to publish the book. I wanted it available for sale in September, because Pope John Paul II was coming to the United States in October. "Now let's figure out how we can make that happen," I said.

I asked eight freelance editors to provide me with twenty diverse and readable short excerpts from the pope's writings. By the first week of March, I had received 120 usable selections. I arranged them in random order, and *Breakfast with the Pope* was conceived.

In the 1990s, the media generally accepted that publishers could quote papal documents without permission of the Vatican. But I wanted to be sure. I wrote to Archbishop John Foley at the Vatican communications office and asked him if we were clear to publish the book.

Weeks rolled by with no response. Anxiety took hold as I realized the book must get to the printer before August or we would not have books in time for the papal visit. At 6:00 a.m., one morning in July, feeling both exasperation and pressure, I prayed: "Lord, I need Archbishop Foley's letter today. Let it be coming off my fax machine when I am done praying."

As I walked across the family room to my office, the fax began to buzz. It was the letter! The archbishop said we needed no permission to publish *Breakfast with the Pope*.

The Lord had made me wait for his response, but he came through. He was training me in both faith and patience.

— *Bert Ghezzi*

CHAPTER 14

Unanswered Prayers

In a popular country song entitled "Unanswered Prayers," Garth Brooks recalls praying that he would marry his high school sweetheart, but it didn't work out. Years later, he met his old girlfriend, and she wasn't the "angel" that he remembered. He thanked God for not answering his prayer!

Catholics believe that God answers prayers, but God does not always give us what we want. We are not healed. Someone we love dies. We do not get the new job, or we lose the job we had. Our home is not protected in a storm. We begin to feel as if God is ignoring us. We are hoping for an answer, but all we get is silence.

Sometimes, no matter how much we pray, things seem to get worse instead of better. More problems. More struggles. More disappointments. We wonder why God does not answer our prayers.

It helps when we realize that we are not alone in our experience of "unanswered prayers." In the Garden of Gethsemane, Jesus asks God to spare him from the painful events he is about to endure, but then Jesus adds, "Not my will, but yours, be done" (Luke 22:42).

God did not stop the crucifixion and death of Jesus, but God triumphed over death when Jesus rose on Easter Sunday. Do we have enough faith to believe that something good will happen — even if our specific prayers appear to go unanswered? Do we have enough trust to believe that God will take care of us? Do we have enough perseverance to continue praying in our darkest moments, with the hope that God will give us enough light to take one step at a time?

Pope Francis urges us to persist in prayer, even if it seems as if our prayer has not been answered. "All of us experience moments of fatigue and discouragement, especially when our prayers seem ineffective," he explains. "God promptly answers his children, although this does not mean he does it in the time and manner that we would like. Prayer is not a magic wand!"

The real purpose of prayer is to establish and preserve our relationship with God, to strengthen our faith, and trust God — even when we don't fully comprehend God's will. The stories in this chapter illustrate some unanswered prayers that led to new spiritual insights and better understanding.

The Prayers God Did Not Answer

More than half the time my prayers for a specific request go unanswered. But that does not stop me from telling God what I think I need. I know that his love for me is all-inclusive. He cares for everything about me and knows how to give me what I really need. When answers don't come, I remind myself of something that C. S. Lewis once said, that we will spend a lot of time in eternity thanking God for those prayers of ours he did not answer!

— *Bert Ghezzi*

Pondering Things in My Heart

Our daughter had a very aggressive breast cancer. She battled it for a little over three years, and she died when she was forty-two.

I always had a foreboding about my daughter from the time she was diagnosed. I lived with that dread on one hand, and hope on the other hand. My husband and I prayed for hope all the time, and God honored that. Every time I would feel dread, God would send a person or a story our way that would give us hope.

My prayer was, "Lord, I don't want her to see how horrible I feel inside, and how sad, and how anxious. I want to be a person of hope and faith so she will want to be with me."

I could never be with my own mother when I was sick because she would cry all the time. I wanted to be strong and courageous and to give my daughter hope. God honored that request, and I am grateful.

When she died, it was like part of my soul died. I went to Our Lady for help, and I finally learned what pondering things in your heart really meant. I realized it was very prideful of me to say to God, "Not thy will, but my will be done." That's really what I was doing. I realized finally that God said no to his Son, and he said no to the mother of his Son. It occurred to me that Mary must have been praying her heart out for her Son, too. If God can say no to her, why can't he say no to me?

— *Carolyn McLean*

I Don't Have an Answer

My son is a Marine, and when he was sent to the Middle East, the fear that something might happen to him was overwhelming. I prayed constantly that he would not be injured. One day I talked to a priest about all of this, and he told me, "You don't think that God will change the direction of a bullet because of your prayers, do you?"

Well, yes, I did believe that because of my prayers my son might be protected in some way. At the same time, it troubled me that other mothers were also praying for their sons or daughters, and their children were killed or wounded.

I am grateful that my son came home safely. Does that mean my prayers were answered and another mother's prayers were not answered? I don't have an answer to this.

— *Veronica Cavan*

PRAYER FOR OUR TROOPS

Lord, hold our troops in your loving hands. Protect them as they protect us. Bless them and their families for the selfless acts they perform for us in our time of need. I ask this in the name of Jesus, our Lord and Savior. Amen.

Waiting for God to Talk to Me

My prayers are basically the prayers I learned when I was a kid. I still say some Latin prayers from when I was an altar boy, but I have also added prayers that I learned since. I always end with a laundry list of people who I pray for — living and dead.

For a long time, I was praying for a very good friend of mine who had cancer. About four years ago, he had a stem-cell transplant with his own stem cells that seemed to work, but then a new kind of cancer came upon him. We had a lot of people praying for him. He had another stem-cell transplant, but a few months later, we lost him at age sixty-one.

He was a wonderful person, a wonderful family man. He took care of so many people all the time. He was always gracious — a firm believer in God. And we lost him. Now I'm asking the question: Why do we lose someone who was not only very close to us, but was also a very productive member of society? Sometimes when I go to Eucharistic Adoration, I wait for God to talk back to me. Maybe I'm just not communicating the right way, because as far as getting an answer about my friend, I'm just not hearing anything. So I continue to pray because I think it's good for me to do that. I rationalize it by telling myself that we all have to die sometime, and maybe God had a need for him. At least I have the lasting memory of our friendship.

— *Joe Smyth*

WHY? WHY? WHY?

When someone we love dies, asking "Why?" is our attempt to make sense out of something that we cannot comprehend. Some "why" questions have answers, but many do not. Sometimes, the question "Why?" is not really a question, but an expression of helplessness, protest, or pain. For some people, "why" questions become a powerful prayer. Like Job, they cry, "Let the Almighty answer me!" (Job 31:35). In time, they discover, as Job did, that God is with us — even if he does not answer our questions.

Die to Yourself and Live for God

After four years of marriage, my husband and I were elated to find that I was pregnant!!! The pregnancy went great. We couldn't wait to hold that baby in our arms.

On the evening of Good Friday, my water broke, and we went to the hospital. Unfortunately, the delivery didn't happen quickly or easily. Unbeknownst to me, the doctor informed my husband that the baby had anencephaly, or absence of a brain.

The baby would only live for a short time. The doctor recommended that I not be told until after the birth.

Thirty-six hours later our son was born, on Easter Sunday. He lived for thirteen hours. My doctor was very compassionate and advised us not to see him. Not knowing what to do, we followed his advice, but it was the worst thing a new mom and dad could do.

I have two memories of our first-born. I remember the nurse telling me he had a beautiful face and body, and the funeral director giving me the crucifix that was on his tiny casket. That was it. His nursery was dismantled before I arrived home, as if a baby had never been expected. I felt as if all my prayers for my baby had gone unanswered.

Unfortunately, the kind doctor also advised my husband not to talk to me about the baby. My heart was broken. I sobbed and sobbed. I just couldn't do what everyone seemed to want me to do. I could not put this experience away and get on with life. My husband felt terrible, but he was afraid to tell me. He listened and held me, but I was inconsolable.

One night Jim started to pray the Rosary. I must have drifted off to sleep, and the next thing I remember was waking up and the room was in a soft glow of light. I heard a voice say, "You will die to yourself and live for me from now on."

I had no idea what "die to yourself" meant. I had never heard that term before, but a peace came over me, and my grief was somewhat lessened from that day on. I was on a lonely journey, but my faith seemed to grow by leaps and bounds. I felt as if God was with me, and he knew my heart.

I had been a labor and delivery nurse before Jimmy's birth, and I tried going back to work, but it was too painful. Instead, I taught nursing until after my second child was born. She was a girl. Thirteen months later another son was born, followed by another daughter.

Eventually, I went back to being a labor and delivery nurse because I knew it was my true calling. When a mom and dad lost a baby, God kept reminding me of what I would have liked when Jimmy was born. I felt called to help these grieving parents. I encouraged them to hold their child. I gave them a picture and the blanket the baby was wrapped in.

When the hospital where I was working closed its obstetrics unit, I joined the staff at another hospital. God led me to this place where I was asked to start a perinatal bereavement service. From there I was invited to hold a training conference for perinatal loss. Many doctors thought I was crazy at first, but I forged on, knowing that our son was behind all this. In time, the physicians and staff saw how much better parents were doing after a loss when we allowed them to hold onto memories of their child. In time, I helped to start support groups for parents and grandparents who had lost a child. And through all of this, I learned what it meant to die to myself and live for God.

— *Kathleen Skipper*

It's What God Gave Us

My son died at age twenty-nine from a heroin overdose. At first impression, it makes him seem like a loser coming from questionable parenting, but nothing could be further from the truth. We were the "perfect" family — church, scouting, baseball, and a lot of love. Michael had a wonderful relationship with his dad. Hockey was their shared passion — both playing and watching.

At age twelve, Michael took a turn and followed a downward spiral. Counseling, love, and prayers were no help. All that being said, Michael didn't hit his bottom until eighteen months before he died. He was sent to drug court and mandated to a live-in facility for thirty days. During that time, we reconnected with him. We shared our feelings, and we learned so much about Michael and his struggles. Heroin is an insidious drug.

When Michael was released, we were all optimistic that drugs were in our past. Michael finished college and met a wonderful girl. We thought our prayers had been answered, but it was not to be. Michael relapsed, got bad street heroin, and died in the college library waiting for his girlfriend.

Those eighteen months when he was clean were wonderful, and I felt that my prayers were answered. Michael reconnected with his sister, Stacey, and his nieces, and with us. We were able to spend time together, which was wonderful. Of course, the outcome was not what I wanted or even expected, but it's what God gave us. Those eighteen months were our gift from God. They gave us the strength to endure Michael's death.

— *Maryann Szafran*

A PRAYER FOR THE HEALING OF ADDICTION

God of Love and Mercy, give us the grace we need to understand addiction. Allow us to see that addiction is a disease. Help us to find ways to halt the growing epidemic of addiction in our society.

Open the eyes of those who are struggling with addiction so that they can recognize their need for help. Give them the strength they need to seek treatment.

For those who are in recovery, protect them from any influences that might jeopardize their sobriety.

Shower your love on the families and friends of people who are struggling with addiction. Give them the patience, the courage, and the faith they need to help their loved one. Guide everyone in the family in their attempts to seek and find lasting peace.
We ask this through Jesus Christ, our Lord. Amen.

CHAPTER 15

When Someone Is Dying

Anyone who has ever kept a vigil at the deathbed of a loved one understands the profound spiritual link that forms as the person transitions from this world into the next.

You don't need a priest to pray for someone who is dying. Sometimes family members gather at the person's bedside to pray silently or out loud. As you will see from the stories in this chapter, traditional Catholic prayers such as the Our Father, the Hail Mary, the Rosary, and the Divine Mercy Chaplet are always good choices. Reading a Scripture passage or praying one of the psalms can have a calming effect. Sometimes it helps to sing or to have sacred music playing softly in the background.

It is not easy when someone you love is dying. "Illness, above all grave illness, always places human existence in crisis and brings with it questions that dig deep," Pope Francis admits. "Our first response may at times be one of rebellion: Why has this happened to me? We can feel desperate, thinking that all is lost, that things no longer have meaning.... In these situations, faith in God is on the one hand tested, yet at the same time can reveal all of its positive resources. Not because faith makes illness, pain, or the questions which they raise, disappear, but because it offers a key by which we can discover the deepest meaning of what we are experiencing; a key that helps us to see how illness can be the way to draw nearer to Jesus who walks at our side, weighed down by the Cross. And this key is given to us by Mary, our Mother, who has known this way at first hand."

Death is an end to a person's earthly existence, but it is the beginning of a person's eternal life with God. The stories in this chapter illustrate the powerful role that prayer plays when someone is dying.

THE SACRAMENT OF THE SICK

Since ancient times, the Catholic Church has maintained a tradition of anointing the seriously ill and the dying. This special anointing was eventually established as a sacrament called "extreme unction," and was commonly referred to as "last rites" for people who were dying. This association of the sacrament with death resulted in some families not calling a priest until the person was unconscious because they did not want to upset their loved one. In other cases, families waited until the last possible moment to call a priest as a guarantee that the person would leave this world in a state of grace.

During the Second Vatican Council (1961–1965), the sacrament was revised with emphasis on anointing people whenever they are seriously ill. The *Catechism of the Catholic Church* explains:

> The proper time for receiving this holy anointing has certainly arrived when the believer begins to be in danger of death because of illness or old age.
>
> Each time a Christian falls seriously ill, he may receive the Anointing of the Sick, and also when, after he has received it, the illness worsens.

Today, the Anointing of the Sick is frequently offered in nursing homes, hospitals, and at communal parish services. It is possible for a priest to administer the sacrament at the bedside of someone who is dying, but most priests prefer that families not wait until death is imminent.

The Grace of Final Perseverance

I was a seminarian, at home on vacation, when our neighbors called and said their mother was dying. They asked if I could come over.

"Sure, I can come," I said, "but I am not a priest. I can't do anything sacramentally."

They just wanted someone to come. So I went to their house, and their mother was in the agony of dying. She didn't want to let go. You could see it on her face. I remembered Jesus saying in the diary of Saint Faustina that if you pray the Chaplet of Divine Mercy at the bedside of someone who is dying, that person will be given the grace of final perseverance.

So I suggested that we pray the Chaplet. The family didn't even know what it was, and I didn't want to make them feel pressured. I pulled out my rosary and said, "Don't worry. I'll do it. It just takes five to seven minutes."

The family members gathered around while I prayed the Chaplet, and during that prayer we all saw the countenance of this woman change from being in tortured agony to what looked like she was seeing something beautiful. Then right there in front of us, when the Chaplet was done, she took her last breath. Her face was at peace, at rest. It was incredible.

Everyone in that room knew that something profound and supernatural had happened. It was an extremely powerful moment of prayer.

— *Father Donald Calloway, M.I.C.*

HOW TO PRAY THE DIVINE MERCY CHAPLET

Using a Rosary …

- Make the Sign of the Cross with the crucifix.
- On the first bead, repeat three times: "O Blood and Water, which gushed forth from the Heart of Jesus as a fountain of Mercy for us, I trust in you."
- On the next three beads, pray the Our Father, the Hail Mary, and the Apostles' Creed.
- On the fifth bead, pray: "Eternal Father, I offer you the Body and Blood, Soul and Divinity of your dearly beloved Son, our Lord, Jesus Christ, in atonement for our sins and those of the whole world."
- On the first set of ten beads pray, "For the sake of his sorrowful passion, have mercy on us and on the whole world."
- Repeat for the remaining decades, praying the "Eternal Father" prayer on the Our Father beads, and the "For the sake of his sorrowful passion" prayer on each of the Hail Mary beads.
- Conclude by praying three times: "Holy God, Holy Mighty One, Holy Immortal One, have mercy on us and on the whole world."

A Double Sign of God's Love and Mercy

Visiting the sick and homebound was an important part of my ministry when I worked in an inner-city parish. A man named Henry was so grateful that I had brought Communion to his dying brother-in-law that he offered to drive me to the homes of the parishioners. Henry would stay in the car and pray while I visited. We became steadfast friends and I introduced Henry to the Divine Mercy Chaplet.

At that time, I belonged to a prayer group. A few of us decided to select one person and pray the Divine Mercy Chaplet for fifty-four days for that person's conversion. I picked my brother, John, who claimed to be an atheist. Henry did not belong to our prayer group, but he offered to pray the Divine Mercy Chaplet privately for John's conversion.

A few months later John was diagnosed with a malignant brain tumor near the brain stem. He underwent brain surgery, and our prayers were answered when he asked to see a priest in the hospital. But John's prognosis was not good.

The night before John died, I left a relic of Saint Thérèse of Lisieux in his room. The next day, I received a call from Henry inquiring about John. I told him John had passed away that morning. Henry proceeded to tell me that earlier in the morning, while he was having breakfast, a mysterious light rested on a rose that was in a vase on his kitchen table. The light split into red and white rays. Henry could not trace its source. Then Henry's wife entered the kitchen, and again this mysterious light rested on the rose and split into red and white rays.

I knew instantly that the rose was a sign of Saint Thérèse of Lisieux. When the rays of Divine Mercy hit the rose, it was a double sign of God's love and mercy. We were all joyful that John had been so wonderfully received by Jesus.

— *Sister Teresita Richardson, O.S.F.*

"We Lift Up Our Souls"

My husband, Joe, was dying. I was on my way to the hospital, and a song we had sung at Mass kept repeating itself in my brain: "We lift up our souls, O my God."

Joe was in a coma. He was in a Catholic hospital, and they had moved him into a private room that was reserved for dying patients. The family was planning for his death. My brother-in-law was giving me advice about which funeral facility I should call. Sister Ellen was preparing me with kind words.

That evening, most of the family had gathered in Joe's room. The hospital seemed quiet. My son-in-law, Ray, said, "Mother, why don't you sing to Dad because they say the dying often retain their hearing after all other senses go."

I thought of that simple tune that was sung at Mass. So I sang, "We lift up his soul, O my God." Soon everyone in the room was humming it.

All of a sudden, through the large tube that was protruding from Joe's mouth, we heard Joe humming along with us! "Quick," someone said. "Call the nurse!"

The nurse came into the room along with Sister Ellen and Sister Joel. The tube was removed. Sure enough, Joe was singing! We all waited in expectation. Yes! Joe had come out of his coma!

What a miracle! Joe lived for another ten years. Often when talking about their father, one or more of my daughters say, "Remember when Dad was dying, and then he lived!"

— *Nancy Allaire Donohue*

"Your Will Be Done"

I was the primary caregiver for my mother following her diagnosis of Alzheimer's and vascular dementia. As I watched her struggle with the disease and its inevitable progression toward death in slow motion, I pleaded many times for God to take her and end her suffering. I also prayed that God would provide a peaceful death for her.

I questioned the mysticism of suffering, asking God why Mom should have to suffer when she was such a good woman. Soul-searching questions about my own life surfaced, such as,

"What does my faith mean to me and how has it sustained me?" "What will give me the strength if I am ever diagnosed with Alzheimer's?"

Through prayer and meditation, I came to reconcile that God had a purpose in keeping her alive, and it wasn't in my purview to understand why. I was not the one in control here. I placed my anxieties and fears in his hands and prayed, "Your will be done."

When Mom was in a coma near death, I was blessed to be the family member at her side in the hospital. I made sure that a priest was called to her bedside to give her the last rites. I held her hands while praying aloud the very prayers she taught me as a child. She gently breathed her last breath and went home to meet her Maker. God answered my prayers for Mom's peaceful death!

— *Vicki Kaufmann*

A PRAYER FOR STRENGTH

The following prayer was written by Vicki Kaufmann for family caregivers:

> Dear Lord, some days it feels that my life is broken in so many places. Today is one of those days when I am in a valley of discouragement and pain. My loved one needs me right now. This disease is horrible! I fear I may not make it through without breaking and cracking in more places in my heart.
>
> I recall your words, "I am with you always, until the end of time." This gives me comfort and peace. Cover me with your light and grace. Help me bear my burdens with strength and compassion. Patch me up to carry

on. I pray that my love, devotion, and dedication to my loved one be renewed for today. Lord, I thank you for your love and your faithfulness! Amen.

A Gift of God

When my eighty-four-year-old father was diagnosed with cancer, I decided to pray for him each morning and each evening. I wanted to do so by asking for the assistance of one of the great saints of the Church. After a little research, I discovered a prayer to Saint Anthony of Padua for cancer victims:

> Dear St. Anthony, you recognized Our Lord Jesus as the Divine Healer. In your goodness and kindness, please intercede for *(mention name)* who is suffering from cancer. If it is God's will, I ask that this day the gift of healing be granted to *(name)*. Comfort him/her during times of unbearable pain, and ask our Lord to grant him/her peace and patience in suffering. May God give *(name)* the fullness of life here on earth, or call him/her home to eternal glory forever. Amen.

I prayed this same prayer to Saint Anthony twice a day, and did not tell anyone what I was doing — not even my wife.

During the next six months, my father underwent chemotherapy and radiation. The tumor shrank. But because of his age, and the location of the tumor, surgery to remove it was too risky. Over time, my father's condition deteriorated. Family members took turns sitting with him day and night. At around 2 a.m. on February 18 — Ash Wednesday — it was my turn. I prayed though the night. At 5:49 a.m. — on the first day of Lent — I witnessed my father take his last breath.

The following Saturday, my mother handed me what looked like a tiny booklet, no more than two inches in height. She said my father had carried it in his pocket for many years, but since he had been diagnosed with cancer, he insisted that he always have it on his person. I never knew this about my dad.

The front of the booklet read, "St. Anthony of Padua, Pray for Us." On the inside was a medal and relic of Saint Anthony, along with this prayer:

> St. Anthony, help me experience peace of mind and heart in my present needs. Free me from needless worry and burdensome fears. Grant me unfailing trust and an awareness of God's loving mercy. Amen.

I was stunned. If this had not happened to me, I would not have believed it. But it did happen, and I will never fail to see it as a gift of God by way of my father.

— *Francis J. Beckwith*

CHAPTER 16

The Prayers of Others

For most Catholics, praying for others is second nature. We believe in the Communion of Saints, which means that all of us — living and dead — are connected to one another spiritually. We pray for other people, and other people pray for us.

There is a special name given to prayer for others. It is called intercessory prayer because we are going directly to God to intercede on their behalf. One of the most profound examples of intercessory prayer took place at the Last Supper when Jesus prayed for the disciples. In John 17:9–26, Jesus prayed that his disciples would be protected from evil, that they would be filled with joy, and that they would be sanctified by truth. In this prayer, Jesus also prayed for all of us, asking that everyone who would come to believe because of the witness of the disciples would remain united with Jesus in the Father's love.

Saint James tells us to "pray for one another, that you may be healed" (James 5:16). Saint Paul asked that "prayers, intercessions, and thanksgivings be made for all men, for kings and all who are in high positions, that we may lead a quiet and peaceable life, godly and respectful in every way" (1 Timothy 2:1–2). Saint Paul also thanked the Corinthians for their prayers, which brought many blessings and resulted in many more prayers of thanks being offered to God (2 Corinthians 1:11).

Sometimes, prayer is the only thing we can do for someone else. Sometimes, prayer is the only way other people can help us. But Pope Francis tells us that our prayers for others must be accompanied by strong faith. Our prayer of intercession must be what he calls "a courageous prayer, that struggles to achieve a miracle, not prayers of courtesy, 'Ah, I will pray for you,' I say an Our Father, a Hail Mary and then I forget.... Prayer works wonders, but we have to believe!"

In this chapter, we see some ways that people have prayed for others, and also how those prayers impacted the people who prayed.

"I'm Praying for You"

Prayer has always been a part of my life. I grew up in a very Catholic, Polish family. I did not take prayer for granted, but it was not until my mother died in 1995 that I realized the true impact of prayer.

My dad had died ten years earlier, and my mother was an everyday part of my life. At her wake, I was so empty that I couldn't pray. But so many people came up to me and said, "I'm praying for you."

The prayers of other people carried me through this difficult time, and I know now what a special gift this was. I felt God's loving arms around me, and I accepted his grace through the prayers of the people he surrounded me with.

— *Diane Germain*

A Gift of Prayer

There is a concept of giving that I learned about a long time ago, which is to give a gift anonymously. Not only does the recipient not know who gave the gift, but the giver may or may not ever know what the reaction was. Thus, the giving is done with no expectation of any reward — not even a simple "Thank you."

I decided to apply this concept to prayer a few years ago when I saw the story of a priest whose life had been touched by a huge tragedy. At that moment, I prayed for all involved, but a few days later I decided to take it to another level.

As part of my personal ministry I had already begun to pray for priests every day, so it was a natural decision to pray for this priest. However, at that point it came to me that I was to pray for this man of God every day for the rest of my life. The catch, of course, is that he does not and will never know of this daily gift.

— *Helen A. Scieszka, Ph.D.*

She Prayed a Rosary for Me Every Day

I have worked in our office at my parish for over twenty years. There was a lady in our parish who I had known all my life, but our personal friendship really bloomed when I was in my fifties and she was approaching one hundred years of age. She called me at the parish office one day to tell me that she prayed a Rosary for me every day. She figured I needed it for my job.

She told me that since she could no longer be out and about, and was pretty much confined to her home unless someone came to take her out, praying her Rosary was all she could do. She prayed all day long, beginning before she got out of bed, in the kitchen, in the living room. She is now praying from heaven. But she became my inspiration for growing a better prayer life.

— *Susan Stout*

Sending up Prayers for Kathy

During the course of a CT scan done to find the cause of my wife Kathy's ongoing stomach pain, the radiologist noticed a tiny, pea-sized growth in her small intestine. Our next-door neighbor promptly brought Kathy a prayer card to Saint Peregrine, the patron saint of cancer patients. We all began praying. Through a precision laparoscopic surgery, the cancer detected on Kathy's scan was successfully removed.

A few months later, I was invited to teach a psychology course at Aquinas College in Nashville, Tennessee, run by the Congregation of the Dominican Sisters of St. Cecilia. Though I had not taught in eight years, and was busy with my job in addition to writing and speaking, I just could not tell the sisters no! I immediately got to work preparing a course to be taught during three weekends that fall.

Kathy's cancer was unusual in that the only direct treatment is surgery. Signs of its return can be detected by a blood test, so Kathy began a quarterly series of lab tests. Not long after the surgery, her numbers began to rise. By mid-summer a new CT scan showed three small tumors in her lymph nodes. This was not a good sign. She needed another surgery. This time it would require a major incision and a bowel resection.

The surgery went well. My class was to begin in just a few weeks. I wanted to tell the sisters I could not teach, but Kathy insisted I do so. I could travel down to Nashville the first weekend without her. Our adult sons would care for her, and she promised to join me for the next two weekends.

From the minute I informed the Nashville Dominicans of Kathy's situation, they unleashed their powers of prayer on her behalf. Even so, a few months later, we were alarmed when Kathy's laboratory values began to rise again. We obtained a second opinion from an oncologist at a major hospital, who advised

Kathy to avoid certain foods before her blood tests to rule out false-positive results. The next time her labs were tested, they were in the completely normal range, where they have remained ever since.

We are thankful to God that Kathy has shown no signs now in almost four years. We prayed for healing and also for guidance in making the right decisions regarding her medical and surgical treatment. And we were buoyed by the knowledge that family, friends, and the Nashville Dominicans were sending up prayers for her.

— *Kevin Vost, Psy.D.*

SAINT PEREGRINE LAZIOSI (1265–1345)

After receiving a vision in which Christ reached out and touched a cancerous ulcer on his leg, Saint Peregrine was healed of his own cancer. He is a patron saint of cancer patients.

Prayer to Saint Peregrine

O great Saint Peregrine, you have been called "The Mighty," "The Wonder-Worker," because of the numerous miracles which you have obtained from God for those who have had recourse to you. For so many years you bore in your own flesh this cancerous disease that destroys the very fiber of our being, and who had recourse to the source of all grace when the power of man could do no more. You were favored with the vision of Jesus coming down from his cross to heal your affliction. Ask of God and Our Lady, the cure of the sick whom we entrust to you. *(Pause here and silently recall the names of the sick for whom you are praying.)* Aided in this way by your powerful intercession, we shall sing to God, now and for all eternity, a song of gratitude for his great goodness and mercy. Amen.

Baby Steps

My husband, Doug, grew up as a Methodist. I am a cradle Catholic. Doug has always supported me in my faith, and I never pressured him to join the Church. As our three daughters grew up, he helped with transportation for religious education and attended all their sacramental milestones. Because of a job transfer, we lived in the South for a while. At that time, he saw I needed extra support, and of his own will, he began attending Sunday Mass with us as a family. He did not verbally participate in song and prayer; he would sit and stand, but never kneel.

After we moved back to Fort Wayne, Indiana, my faith grew. I began going to daily Mass and joined several prayer groups, always praying for Doug's conversion. My friend Karen introduced me to a couple of seminarians, who would also pray for him.

A short time later, the Franciscan Brothers Minor opened a monastery in town. Doug met several of the brothers, and they all said, "We will pray for you." During this time, I joined the Saint Monica group in our parish. Every Tuesday we prayed a Rosary for conversions through the intercession of Saint Monica, whose prayers brought about the conversion of her husband and her son Saint Augustine.

After our daughters grew up and left home, Doug continued to go to Sunday Mass with me. One week, our pastor announced that ushers were needed. Doug said, "That's something I can do," and our pastor approved. The beginning of his conversion!

"Baby steps," our parish priest told me, "baby steps."

When my friend Karen joined the cloistered Sisters of Poor Clare, it made a big impression on Doug, knowing that Karen and the other cloistered sisters were praying for our family. He then began attending Mass with me a couple days during the week. He would sit in the main church, listening, as a group of us prayed the Rosary in the chapel before Mass.

One morning before leaving for work, Doug asked me to call the church "and sign me up for RCIA." A few days later, for the first time, Doug knelt beside me and participated in the song and prayer of Mass. It was a very special day, August 15, the feast of the Assumption and the anniversary of my mom's death.

After forty-two years of marriage, Doug was received into the Church the following March. Three months later, we went on a pilgrimage to Italy. It was our "spiritual" honeymoon. Doug's conversion was truly an answer to many prayers.

— *Norma Baisinger*

ST. MONICA SODALITY

In 1995, Father C. Frank Phillips, C.R., pastor of St. John Cantius Parish, in Chicago, believed so strongly in the power of prayer that he started St. Monica Sodality for people in his parish who were praying for the conversion of a family member or friend. The purpose of the Sodality was twofold: to pray for the conversion of loved ones and to provide support for people who have family members or friends in need of conversion. As news of the Sodality spread, people began to send prayer intentions to the parish. Some asked if they could join as long-distance members. Others wanted to start a St. Monica Sodality in their own parish. Today, chapters of St. Monica Sodality have sprung up all over the world.

Prayer to Saint Monica

Gracious and loving God, you inspired St. Monica to set a good example and to pray for the conversion of her family members. Through the intercession of St. Monica, I ask for the grace to be a faithful example to my family members and friends, with the hope that they will turn to you. Help me to love them unconditionally. Keep me from being judgmental. Give me the wisdom to know when to speak and what to say. Allow your Holy Spirit to work through me, as you did with St. Monica, to touch their hearts and minds. I ask this through Jesus Christ, our Lord. Amen.

The Prayers of My Parents

When I was an infant, I could not digest any form of milk. I would reject the liquids and get terribly sick. I was placed on intravenous feedings for months. Through my parents' prayers, I made a slow recovery back to good health, but my immune system was affected.

A few years later, I was diagnosed with alopecia areata, an autoimmune disease that causes hair loss. Again, through the power of prayer and God's holy grace, I regained the growth of my hair. Today, I am able to drink milk and milk products without issues, and I need to go for a haircut frequently due to the beautiful thickness of my hair.

— *Maria Garrity*

We Kept the Baby on the Prayer Line

I was the coordinator of our parish prayer line for twenty years. Just after I started the prayer line, there was a lady who was expecting a baby. Three different doctors recommended to her and her husband that she have an abortion because the baby was not going to live long following birth. They were told that their baby had several fatal problems. We kept this baby on the prayer line throughout the pregnancy. The parents refused the abortion, and their precious little one was born perfect!

— *Nancy Riecke*

PRAYER FOR THE UNBORN

God of love, bless the tiny lives that are carried in the wombs of their mothers. Help us to recognize that these little babies are created in your image and likeness. Open our eyes to the gift of their lives. Protect these tiny babies and their mothers from harm until the joy-filled day of their birth. We ask this through your Son, Jesus Christ, our Lord and our Savior. Amen.

The Lord Healed Him

When my youngest son was little, he was diagnosed with cystic fibrosis. The doctors told us the capillaries in his lungs were starting to plug up and he wouldn't live past his sixteenth birthday. They said they could do this and that if we just put our faith in them.

I said, "Wait a minute. I am a Catholic. I put my trust in the Lord. It's not that I won't listen to you. I believe the Lord put you here at the right time and place for us, but we are also going to rely on the power of prayer. My faith is in the Lord."

When we brought my son home, I called people from our prayer group. They prayed over my son. About a year after the diagnosis, he had no symptoms. The doctors said he had really improved. They were "patting themselves on the back" because they had given him certain medications. I told them that I had stopped giving him the medicine because I didn't want to put this stuff in him if he didn't need it. We weren't doing the chest treatments, either, because he was breathing fine and running around.

The doctors couldn't believe it. My son never had symptoms again. Now he is twenty-six, and he is doing fine. Everyone was saying maybe he never had the disease. I said, "No. The Lord healed him!" And I thank the Lord every day.

— *Mark Piscitello*

Praying Across America

In 2011, I completed a 3,700-mile run from California to New York. My mission was to pray across America and show everyone how the Lord can work in amazing ways in our lives.

Before I started, I set up a website where people could track my progress and send me messages. During my four months on the road, I received prayer requests from all over the world. Each evening, I would write the new prayer intentions on a piece of paper that I carried with me the next day.

As I ran, I prayed Hail Marys on my rosary ring for each intention. I prayed for a missing girl, a baby with a tumor, a man looking for work, a priest with cancer, people with eating disorders, a woman searching for a job, several couples trying to start a family, and many pregnant women. I prayed for a couple who was about to lose their home, and a family whose son was estranged from them. I prayed for lonely people with no family. I promised myself that I would reach out to everyone because even the smallest gestures mean so much to a lonely person.

A friend of mine, who worked as a substance-abuse counselor, told her group about my run. They asked me to pray for them to stay clean and sober, to be forgiven for their actions, and to reconnect with loved ones.

I received prayer requests from many people who struggled financially. I prayed for a young man who could not walk. I offered up my pain and suffering for a little girl who had been emotionally and physically abused. I prayed for a woman whose husband of twenty-three years wanted a divorce. I received a prayer request from someone whose friend was lost and needed God.

I felt saddened about the troubles of the people in my prayers. At the same time, it made me realize that the best thing I could do for them was pray. I said a decade of the Rosary for each cross I passed on the road that marked the place someone had died in an accident. It made me treasure each moment of my life.

I received many requests to pray for our armed forces. One day a military vehicle passed me on the road while I was praying for them! I also prayed for construction crews and for the people in each town I ran through. I loved it when people asked me what I was doing, because it was an opportunity to spread my mission about prayer.

I prayed for my friend Matt, who was studying for the priesthood. I prayed for everyone who was trying to discern a vocation.

At the beginning of my run, I thought this journey would be about me praying for others, but a big portion of it was other people praying for me. I was encouraged by the number of people who sent notes explaining how my run had given them hope and inspired them to pray. I felt so humbled to be involved in the prayer lives of so many people from all over the world.

A teenager asked me to pray for myself. It was a good reminder. I had a direct answer to prayer on one stretch of road when a strong wind suddenly died down. I felt as if God was taking this run with me. I realized how much I loved spending time with God. I often found myself talking to God and telling him my concerns. I started to pray for what the Lord wanted me to do with my life after the run ended.

As I ran and prayed, I began to see how many things I took for granted. I felt thankful for blessings that came my way in the people I met, the prayer intentions I received, and the strength I got from the Lord. Running in a cold rain and being sprayed by passing cars got me down one day, but then I read a prayer intention for the homeless. At least I had money for food and shelter at the end of the day.

Some people let me know how my prayers were answered: a child with cancer went into remission, two couples became pregnant, an elderly woman returned to good health, a child with suspected brain damage was okay, and a lot of people started praying the Rosary.

During the last few miles of my run, prayers of thanksgiving rose up from my innermost spirit. I had started my run touching the warm waters of the Pacific Ocean, and I ended by running into the cold waters of the Atlantic Ocean. It felt like a second baptism as I emerged from the Atlantic a different man than the one who left the Pacific four months earlier. I felt closer to God, and my desire to do his will was so much stronger. I experienced a real sense of God's love. I felt more joy in my life, and I had a totally new outlook. I recognized the blessings in my life. I could look at people with greater compassion. I learned to understand rather than judge. I experienced a deeper devotion to Mary, who helped draw me closer to Christ. I became convinced of the power of prayer.

— *Jeff Grabosky*

Afterword

It is my hope the stories in this book have been an inspiration for you. They have certainly been an inspiration for me. I thank God for all of the wonderful people who shared their prayer experiences. And I pray that all of your prayers will be answered in ways that will bring you joy in accordance with God's love and mercy.

Notes

CHAPTER 1: GOD LISTENS … GOD ANSWERS

Page 13 — **"keeping company with God"**: Saint Clement of Alexandria, *Stromata*, Chapter 7.

Page 13 — **five different forms of prayer**: *Catechism of the Catholic Church*, 2626–2643.

Page 14 — **prayer also plays a role in physical health and emotional stability**: Dr. Herbert Benson, a cardiovascular specialist at Harvard Medical School, identified "the relaxation response" connected with prayer, which resulted in decreased heart rate, lower blood pressure, and more regular breathing patterns. Dr. Andrew Newberg, director of the Center for Spirituality and the Mind at the University of Pennsylvania, discovered that levels of dopamine in the brain increased during prayer, which produced feelings of emotional well-being. A study by J. Schnittker, in the *Journal for the Scientific Study of Religion*, showed prayer helps people cope with life, stress, and depression.

CHAPTER 2: "LORD, TEACH US TO PRAY"

Page 15 — **"the fundamental Christian prayer"**: *Catechism of the Catholic Church*, 2773.

Page 15 — **"the most perfect of prayers"**: Saint Thomas Aquinas, *Summa Theologica*, II-II, 83, 9.

Page 15 — **"In the evening, before going to bed …"** — Pope Francis, General Audience, June 22, 2016, available at https://w2.vatican.va/content/francesco/en/audiences/2016/documents/papa-francesco_20160622_udienza-generale.html.

CHAPTER 3: COME, HOLY SPIRIT

Page 26: — **… the seven gifts of the Spirit …** — *Catechism of the Catholic Church*, 1831.

Page 26 — **"The Holy Spirit is the one who moves us … "**: Pope Francis, Morning Homily, May 9, 2016, available at http://en.radiovaticana.va/news/2016/05/09/pope_the_holy_spirit_makes_us_real_christians,_not_virtual/1228446.

Page 26 — **"guides us in the way to think … "**: Pope Francis, address during the midday *Regina Caeli*, May 1, 2016, available at https://w2.vatican.va/content/francesco/en/angelus/2016/documents/papa-francesco_regina-coeli_20160501.html.

Page 35 — **"so as to make manifest the power …"**: *Catechism of the Catholic Church*, 1508.

CHAPTER 4: "IF TODAY YOU HEAR HIS VOICE …"

Page 38 — **"If today you hear his voice …"**: Excerpts from the *Lectionary for Mass for Use in the Dioceses of the United States of America, second typical edition* © 2001, 1998, 1997, 1986, 1970 Confraternity of Christian Doctrine, Inc., Washington, DC. Used with permission. All rights reserved. No portion of this text may be reproduced by any means without permission in writing from the copyright owner.

Page 38 — **"Speak, Lord, because your servant is listening"**: Pope Francis, Morning Homily, April 14, 2016, available at http://en.radiovaticana.va/news/2016/04/14/be_docile_to_the_holy_spirit_-_pope_francis_at_casa_santa_ma/1222680.

Page 42 — **"Of course, everyone has doubts …"**: Pope Francis, General Audience, November 23, 2016, available at https://w2.vatican.va/content/francesco/en/audiences/2016/documents/papa-francesco_20161123_udienza-generale.html.

Page 44 — **"A child has nothing to give …"**: Pope Francis, Homily in Tbilisi, Georgia, October 1, 2016, available at https://w2.vatican.va/content/francesco/en/homilies/2016/documents/papa-francesco_20161001_omelia-georgia.html.

CHAPTER 5: SIGNS FROM ABOVE

Page 48 — **According to a Pew Forum survey …**: Pew Research Center's Forum on Religion & Public Life, December 2009, available at http://www.pewforum.org/2009/12/09/many-americans-mix-multiple-faiths/#6.

Page 49 — **"he felt his heart touched … "**:Vatican statement on Pope Francis' coat of arms, available at https://w2.vatican.va/content/francesco/en/elezione/stemma-papa-francesco.html.

Page 50 — **"*servants* and messengers of God …"**: *Catechism of the Catholic Church*, 329 (emphasis in original); also see 328, 330–336.

CHAPTER 6: I NEED A MIRACLE!

Page 61 — **Pope Francis tells us that in praying for a miracle …**: Pope Francis, Homily, May 20, 2013, available at http://en.radiovaticana.va/storico/2013/05/20/pope_at_mass_courageous%2C_humble_prayer_can_work_wonders/en1-693742.

Page 68 — **"possible pastoral initiatives for the future" …**: Vatican Secretariat of State press communiqué, February 11, 2017, available at https://press.vatican.va/content/salastampa/en/bollettino/pubblico/2017/02/11/170211a.html.

Page 68 — **"The most striking evidence of the presence of God … "**: Diocese Issues Interim Findings on Miraculous Claims: Statement by Most Rev. Daniel P. Reilly, Bishop of Worcester (January 24, 1999), available at http://www.cesnur.org/testi/Worcester.htm.

CHAPTER 7: OBJECTS OF FAITH

Page 73 — **The *Catechism of the Catholic Church* says the use of a sacramental …**: *Catechism of the Catholic Church*, 1667–1679.

Page 73 — **"I think of the steadfast faith of those mothers … "**: Pope Francis, apostolic exhortation *Evangelii Gaudium*, 125, available at http://w2.vatican.va/content/francesco/en/apost_exhortations

/documents/papa-francesco_esortazione-ap_20131124_evangelii-gaudium.html.

Page 75 — **"From long experience I have learned ... "**: St. Teresa of Ávila, *Autobiography*, Saint Benedict Press, TAN Books, 2009.

CHAPTER 8: PRAYING WITH OUR LADY

Page 83 — **"In our life, we are not alone ... "**: Pope Francis, Angelus address in Sweden's Swedbank Stadium, November 1, 2016, available at https://zenit.org/articles/popes-angelus-in-malmo/.

Page 92 — **"Our act of consecration refers ultimately ... "**: Pope John Paul II, Address to Participants of the Study Week of the Pontifical Academy of Sciences, September 26, 1986, available at https://w2.vatican.va/content/john-paul-ii/en/speeches/1986/september/documents/hf_jp-ii_spe_19860922_simposio-maria-gesu.html.

CHAPTER 9: SAINTS ALIVE!

Page 97 — **"saints are men and women ..."**: Pope Francis, Homily, October 16, 2016, available at http://en.radiovaticana.va//news/2016/10/16/pope_francis_canonizes_seven_new_saints_/1265625.

Page 100 — **"I will let fall a shower of roses"**: Society of the Little Flower, available at www.littleflower.org/therese/.

CHAPTER 10: LEAD ME, LORD

Page 109 — **"Do I pray that the Lord gives me the desire ... "**: Pope Francis, Morning Homily, January 27, 2015, available at http://en.radiovaticana.va/news/2015/01/27/pope_francis__we_must_ask_god_for_the_desire_to_do_his_will/1120206.

Page 113 — **"And I solemnly declare to everyone ..."**: Scripture quotation is taken from the *Holy Bible, New Living Translation*, copyright ©1996, 2004, 2007, 2013, 2015 by Tyndale House Foundation. Used by permission of Tyndale House Publishers, Inc., Carol Stream, Illinois 60188. All rights reserved.

Page 117 — **"Lord, I entrust this to you …"**: Pope Francis, Morning Homily, May 5, 2015, available at http://en.radiovaticana.va/news/2015/05/05/pope_christians_are_not_masochists_because_they_have_hope/1141823.

CHAPTER 11: TO FORGIVE AND TO BE FORGIVEN

Page 118 — **"*Forgiveness* is, above all … "**: Pope Francis, Angelus Address, July 24, 2016, available at https://w2.vatican.va/content/francesco/en/angelus/2016/documents/papa-francesco_angelus_20160724.html (emphasis in original).

Page 121 — **"Real love is about loving … "**: "Pope Francis: meeting with young people in Manila," January 18, 2015, available at http://en.radiovaticana.va/news/2015/01/18/pope_francis_meeting_with_young_people_in_manila/1118765.

CHAPTER 12: MONEY FROM HEAVEN

Page 129 — **"Jesus' outlook is very different … "**: Pope Francis, Angelus Address, June 2, 2013, available at https://w2.vatican.va/content/francesco/en/angelus/2013/documents/papa-francesco_angelus_20130602.html.

Page 129 — **"receives God's gifts gratefully …"**: *Stewardship: A Disciple's Response,* A Pastoral Letter on Stewardship (Washington, D.C.: United States Conference of Catholic Bishops, 2002), p. 9.

Page 129 — **"Money is important, especially when … "**: Pope Francis, address to participants in the meeting "Economy of Communion," sponsored by the Focolare Movement, February 4, 2017, available at https://w2.vatican.va/content/francesco/en/speeches/2017/february/documents/papa-francesco_20170204_focolari.html.

Page 132 — **"I am now completely convinced …"**: Blessed Frédéric Ozanam, available at http://vincentians.com/en/quotes-collection/frederic-ozanam-quotes/.

CHAPTER 13: WITHOUT A DOUBT

Page 138 — **"We must look back and remember …"**: Pope Francis, Morning Homily, April 21, 2016, available at http://en.radiovaticana.va/news/2016/04/21/pope__we_must_memorize_god%E2%80%99s_beautiful_deeds_in_our_lives/1224466.

CHAPTER 14: UNANSWERED PRAYERS

Page 148 — **"All of us experience moments of fatigue and discouragement … ":** Pope Francis, General Audience, May 25, 2016, available at http://en.radiovaticana.va/news/2016/05/25/pope_francis_perseverance_prayer_needed_magic_wand/1232338.

Page 148 — **C. S. Lewis once said … :** C. S. Lewis, "Petitionary Prayer" (1953) in *Christian Reflections*, Walter Hooper, ed. (Grand Rapids, MI: Wm. B. Eerdmans Publishing Co., 1967).

CHAPTER 15: WHEN SOMEONE IS DYING

Page 156 — **"Illness, above all grave illness, always places human existence in crisis … ":** Message of His Holiness Pope Francis for the 24th World Day of the Sick, September 15, 2015, available at https://w2.vatican.va/content/francesco/en/messages/sick/documents/papa-francesco_20150915_giornata-malato.html.

Page 157 — **"The proper time for receiving this holy anointing … ":** *Catechism of the Catholic Church*, 1528–1529.

CHAPTER 16: THE PRAYERS OF OTHERS

Page 166 — **"a courageous prayer, that struggles to achieve a miracle … ":** Pope Francis, Morning Homily, May 20, 2013, available at http://en.radiovaticana.va/storico/2013/05/20/pope_at_mass_courageous%2C_ humble_prayer_can_ work_wonders/en1-693742.

Also by
Lorene Hanley Duquin

GRIEVING THE LOSS OF A LOVED ONE:
DAILY MEDITATIONS
Powerful one-page meditations that will help you work through the various aspects of grieving, as they did for the author herself. Rooted in prayer, inspired by the Holy Spirit, and conveying important life lessons.
ID# T1862

WHEN A LOVED ONE LEAVES THE CHURCH
An engaging blend of stories from real people, Church teaching, sociological studies, and plain old common sense bring comfort and understanding to those who bear the burden of having a loved one leave the Faith.
ID# 940

RECOVERING FAITH:
STORIES OF CATHOLICS WHO CAME HOME
Personal and heartfelt faith journeys of 18 well-known Catholics who came back to their faith. You'll be fascinated and encouraged by the way Christ touched each one to bring them all home.
ID# T1137

TO ORDER FROM OUR SUNDAY VISITOR
Call: 800-348-2440
Fax: 800-498-6709
Online: OSV.com